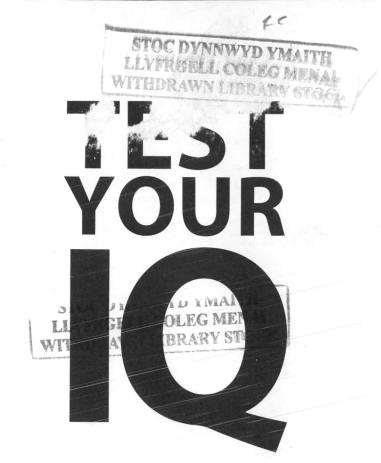

TEST YOUR IQ

400 questions to
boost your brainpower

2nd edition

Philip Carter

LONDON PHILADELPHIA NEW DELHI

Whilst the author has made every effort to ensure that the content of this book is accurate, please note that occasional errors can occur in books of this kind. If you suspect that an error has been made in any of the tests included in this book, please inform the publishers at the address printed below so that it can be corrected at the next reprint.

Publisher's note
Every possible effort has been made to ensure that the information contained in this book is accurate at the time of going to press, and the publishers and author cannot accept responsibility for any errors or omissions, however caused. No responsibility for loss or damage occasioned to any person acting, or refraining from action, as a result of the material in this publication can be accepted by the editor, the publisher or the author.

First published in Great Britain and the United States in 2000 by Kogan Page Limited
Reprinted 2001, 2004
Reissued 2007
Reprinted 2007
Second edition 2009
Reprinted 2012

120 Pentonville Road
London N1 9JN
United Kingdom
www.koganpage.com

1518 Walnut Street, Suite 1100
Philadelphia PA 19102
USA

ISBN 978 0 7494 5677 1

British Library Cataloguing-in-Publication Data

A CIP record for this book is available from the British Library.

Library of Congress Cataloging-in-Publication Data
Carter, Philip J.
    Test your IQ : 400 questions to boost your brainpower / Philip Carter. — 2nd ed.
        p. cm.
    ISBN 978-0-7494-5677-1
1. Intelligence tests. 2. Self-evaluation. I. Title.
    BF431.3.C3726 2009
    153.9'3--dc22
                                                            2009017057

Typeset by Saxon Graphics Ltd, Derby
Printed and bound in India by Replika Press Pvt Ltd

Contents

Introduction

Intelligence is the ability to respond adaptively to new situations, to think abstractly and to comprehend complex ideas. IQ is the abbreviation for Intelligence Quotient. The word quotient means the number of times that one number will divide into another. An intelligence test (IQ Test) is a standardized test designed to measure human intelligence as distinct from attainments.

The measured IQ of children is equal to mental age divided by actual (chronological) age. For example, if a child of eight years of age obtains a score expected of a ten-year-old, the child will have a measured IQ of 125, by means of the following calculation:

$$\frac{\text{Mental age}}{\text{Chronological age}} \times 100 = IQ$$

or

$$\frac{10}{8} \times 100 = 125 \text{ IQ}$$

This method of calculating IQ does not apply to adults because beyond the age of 18 there is little or no improvement in mental development. Adults, therefore, have to be judged on an IQ test in which the average score is 100. The results are graded above and below this norm according to known test scores.

The tests that have been compiled for this book have not been standardized, so an actual IQ assessment cannot be given. However, at the end of this Introduction there is a guide to assessing your performance in each test and also a cumulative guide for your overall performance on all ten tests.

The tests are intended as valuable practice for readers who may have to take an IQ test in the future, and they will also help to increase your vocabulary and to develop your powers of calculation and logical reasoning. The questions are challenging, and deliberately so, as this is the only way to boost your performance and increase your brainpower.

The book consists of ten separate tests for you to attempt, each of 40 questions. Each test is of approximately the same degree of difficulty. A time limit of **90 minutes** is allowed for each test. The correct answers are given at the end of the book, and you should award yourself one point for each correct answer.

Use the following tables to assess your performance:

One test

Score	Rating
36–40	Exceptional
31–35	Excellent
25–30	Very good
19–24	Good
14–18	Average

Ten tests

Score	Rating
351–400	Exceptional
301–350	Excellent
241–300	Very good
181–240	Good
140–180	Average

Test One

1. Create two words using the following ten letters each once only.

   Clue: grand tune (4, 6)

   MYSEVODLTA

2. Which is the odd one out?

   ISTHMUS, FJORD, ATOLL, POLDER, ARCHIPELAGO

3. What number should replace the question mark?

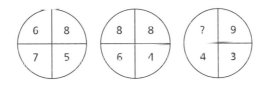

4. CARTON, ENJOYMENT, WORDSMITH
   Which of the following words continues the above sequence?

   COPY, REEF, COPE, REST, ACHE

5. Comparison

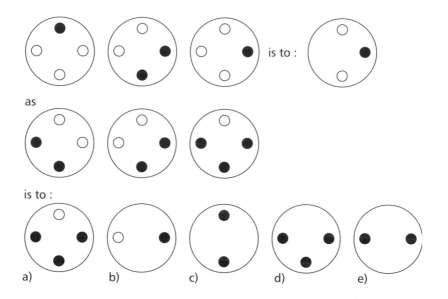

6. What word in brackets means the same as the word in capitals?

FORTE (endowment, conduct, talent, redoubt, style)

7. What number comes next in this sequence?

25, 32, 27, 36, ?

8. Place two letters in each bracket so that these finish the word on the left and start the word on the right. The letters in the brackets, read downwards in pairs, will spell out a six-letter word.

Clue: blue-pencil

FA (. .) SK
HO (. .) AN
KI (. .) AR

9. A car travels at a speed of 40 mph over a certain distance and then returns over the same distance at a speed of 60 mph. What is the average speed for the total journey?

10. Spiral clockwise round the perimeter to spell out a nine-letter word, which must finish in the centre square. The word commences at one of the corner squares. You must provide the missing letters.

	N	
B	E	A
A	C	N

11. MEANDER: WIND
    TRAVERSE: a) stampede
              b) forward
              c) across
              d) retrace
              e) towards

12. What familiar phrase is indicated below?

13. Comparison

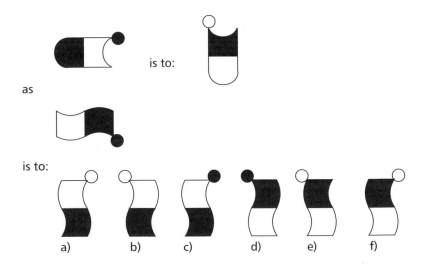

14. The following is an anti-magic square, where none of the horizontal, vertical or corner-to-corner lines totals 34. It is possible, however, by moving the position of just four of the numbers to convert this into a true magic square, where each horizontal, vertical and corner-to-corner line adds up to 34.

    Can you make the necessary corrections?

4	14	8	1
9	16	6	12
5	11	10	15
7	2	3	13

15. What do the following words have in common?

    LEGUMES, QUASHED, AFFIRMS, CLOAKED

16. What number should replace the question mark?

    926 : 24
    799 : 72
    956 : ?

17. Solve the three anagrams to complete a quotation by Confucius.

    Clue: Save something for a rainy day.

    WHEN   P . . .P . . . . .   C . . . ., . . N . .

                     ↑SOPPY TRIER↑   ↑DEMON COOTS↑

    . . E A . . . .   IT.

    ↑ FOUL ALES ↑

18. Add one letter, not necessarily the same letter, to each word at the front, end or middle to find two words that are opposite in meaning.

    LOG PITY

19. What number should replace the question mark?

7	10	9	6
5	1	3	7
2	3	2	1
4	12	8	?

20. What well-known proverb is opposite in meaning to the one below?

    Beware of Greeks bearing gifts.

21. If meat in a river (3 in 6) is T(HAM)ES can you find the path in a celestial body (4 in 6)?

22. In the two numerical sequences below, one number that appears in the top sequence should appear in the bottom sequence and vice versa. Which two numbers should be changed round?

    10, 20, 31, 43, 54, 70

    10, 18, 28, 40, 56, 70

23. Which is the odd one out?

    a) ⊐ ⊔⊐ ⊢⊐ ⊐ ⊢=⊣ ⌐

    b) ⊐ ⊔⊐ ⊢=⊐ ⊐ ⊢⊣ ⌐

    c) ⊐ ⊢=⊐ ⊐ ⊢⊣ ⌐⊐ ⊔

    d) ⊐ ⊢⊣ ⌐⊐ ⊔⊐ ⊢=⊐

    e) ⊣ ⌐⊐ ⊔⊐ ⊢=⊐⊐ ⊢

24. 6 2 H N F 7 3 P L 9 K

    Arrange the letters in forward alphabetical order followed by the numbers in descending order.

25.

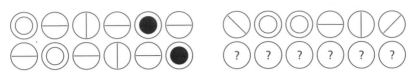

Which set of symbols should replace the question marks?

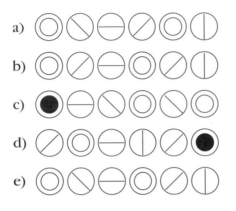

26. Place a word in the brackets that means the same as the definitions outside the brackets.

ringlet   (   )   clasp

27. The top set of six numbers has a relationship to the set of six numbers below. The two sets of six boxes on the left have the same relationship as the two sets of six boxes on the right.

5	9	2	22	13	7		12	3	4	15	10	6
10	18	1	11	26	14		?	?	?	?	?	?

Which set of numbers should, therefore, replace the question marks?

a)

24	6	2	30	20	5

b)

24	9	8	26	5	12

c)

6	12	2	30	20	12

d)

9	9	8	26	20	3

e)

6	6	2	30	5	3

28. Complete the two eight-letter words reading clockwise which must be similar in meaning.

    In each word you must find the starting point and provide the two missing letters.

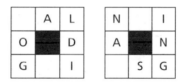

29. A man weighs 75% of his own weight plus 39 lbs. How much does he weigh?

30. ► ╫ ■ $ ⅃⅃ & £ Є ↕ ∑ ► ╫ ■ $ ⅃⅃ & £ Є ↕ ∑ ► ╫ ■ £ Є ↕ ∑ ► ╫ ■ $ ⅃⅃ & £ Є ↕ ∑ ► ╫ ■ $ ⅃⅃ & £ Є ↕ ∑

Which three symbols are missing from the above sequence and from where within the sequence are they missing?

a) ∑ ► ╫

b) $ ⅃⅃ &

c) ╫ ■ $

d) ⅃⅃ & ∑

e) ⅃⅃ & £

31. 36, 429, 32, 57, 52, 392, 46, ?
What number should replace the question mark?

32. A sample of eight gizmos is known to contain three defective gizmos. What is the probability of selecting three defective gizmos in the first three selections?

33. Select two words that are synonyms, plus an antonym of these two synonyms, from the list of words below.

optical, vigilant, rotund, manifest, remiss, feasible, circumspect

34. Complete the equation by correctly identifying the missing part of the calculation from the list of options below.

$$\frac{60 \times (\,?\,)}{(3 \times 2)^2} = \frac{6^3}{492 - 276}$$

   a) 60%
   b) $\dfrac{2}{5}$
   c) 0.65
   d) 0.75

35. Change one letter only in each word below to form a familiar phrase.

   AID THEY SORE

36.

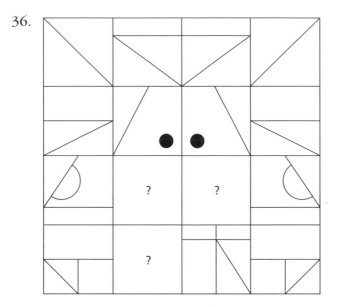

Which is the missing section?

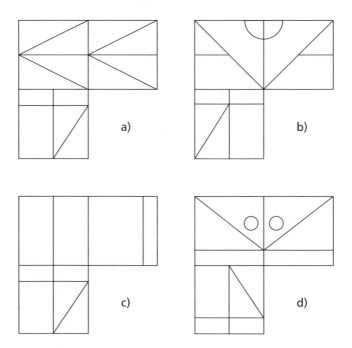

a)

b)

c)

d)

37. Identify two words (one from each set of brackets) that form a connection (analogy), thereby relating to the words in capitals in the same way.

    CHISEL   (cut, smooth, tool)

    AUGER   (engrave, drill, punch)

38. How many minutes is it before 12 noon if 48 minutes ago it was three times as many minutes past 9 am?

39. What letter is two below the letter immediately to the left of the letter which is immediately below the letter two to the right of the letter A?

A	B	C	D	E	
F	G	H	I	J	
K	L	M	N	O	
P	Q	R	S	T	
U	V	W	X	Y	Z

40. break   bottle   rough

    Which word below has something in common with all the words above?

    donkey, rabbit, turtle, ox, tortoise

Test Two

1. How many lines appear below?

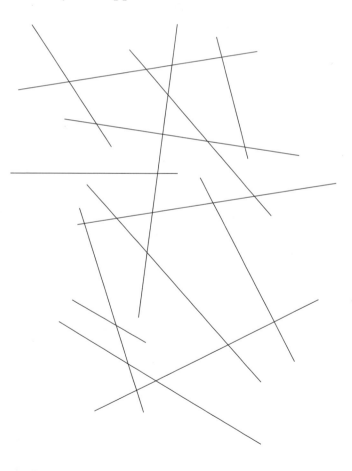

2. Susceptible to attack or damage.

    Which word below most closely fits the above definition?

    DEBILITATED, VULNERABLE, UNSTABLE,
    EMASCULATED, UNPREPARED

3. SUNDAY
    MONDAY
    TUESDAY
    WEDNESDAY
    THURSDAY
    FRIDAY
    SATURDAY
    SUNDAY

    Which day is three days before the day immediately
    following the day two days before the day three days after
    the day immediately before Friday?

4. Change one letter only in each word below to find a well-
    known phrase.

    ON TIE WINK

5. Spiral clockwise to spell out a 10-letter word that starts
    and finishes with the same two letters. You must provide
    the missing letter.

6. Insert the letters provided into the spaces to spell out a palindromic phrase, that is, one that reads the same backwards and forwards.

   Clue: exercise franchise

   TREE VISITOR

   . . S . . . . . O . . . . . .

7. Squares

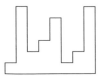

   Which of the following pieces, when fitted to the above piece, will form a perfect square?

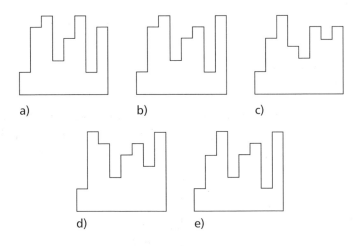

   a)   b)   c)

   d)   e)

8. On glancing through your morning newspaper you notice that four pages are missing. One of the missing pages is page 8. The back page of the newspaper is 28. What are the other three missing pages?

9. Which of the following is not an anagram of a type of book?

NEIL COX
ASSURE HUT
SUMO BIN
SACK OBOE
ROY COKE

10. Which word in brackets is opposite in meaning to the word in capitals?

SIGNIFICANT (ordinary, stupid, modest, petty, dull)

11. FELINE: CAT
    VULPINE: a) ferret
              b) fox
              c) deer
              d) wolf
              e) sheep

12. What number should replace the question mark?

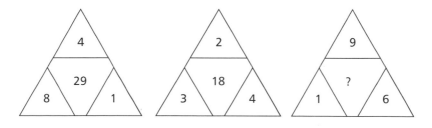

13. Find two words, one in the first grid and one in the second, that are antonyms. The words can be read backwards, forwards, horizontally, vertically or diagonally, but always in a straight line.

T	E	D	Y	T
R	R	U	L	S
Y	A	A	P	A
S	H	R	P	L
T	S	F	A	B

H	I	M	S	P
P	R	P	M	A
A	A	A	T	S
T	R	A	T	S
T	E	M	A	S

14. Odd one out

Which of A, B, C, D or E is the odd one out?

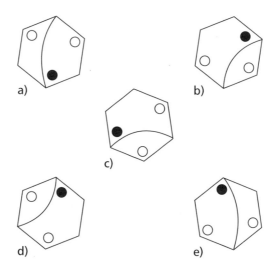

15. Arrange the following words in a line so that each pair of words in the line forms a new word or phrase:

for example: word, game, pass, point = pass, word, game, point to give the words or phrases, password, word game and game-point.

SHORT, GROUP, WATER, LINE, STORY, AGE, FRESH, FALL

16. Which two numbers come next in this sequence?

38, 24, 62, 12, 74, ?

17. Which is the odd one out?

ROOSTER, BUCK, GANDER, PEN, RAM

18. The following is extracted from which hyphenated word?

Clue: viewing area

. . . . . R E-G A . . . . .

19. Which two numbers should replace the question marks?

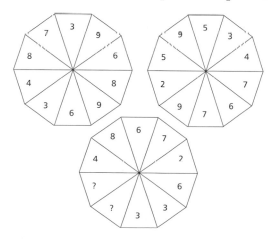

20. OUTLINE TAX is an anagram of which 10-letter word?

21.
	32148	is to	18324
and	39522	is to	23529
and	61194	is to	14196
therefore	66762	is to	?

22. What letter is two to the right of the letter immediately below the letter which is two to the right of the letter immediately above the letter K?

A	B	C	D	E	
F	G	H	I	J	
K	L	M	N	O	
P	Q	R	S	T	
U	V	W	X	Y	Z

23. ☼ ♀ ☺ ♂ ▲ ─ ◀ ▼ ☺ ♀ ■ ▲ ☼ ♀ ☺ ♂ ▲ ─ ◀ ▼ ☺ ♀ ■
▲ ♪ ☼ ♀ ☺ ♂ ▲ ─ ◀ ▼ ☺ ♀ ■ ▲ ♪ ☼ ♀ ☺ ♂ ▲ ─ ◀
▼ ☺ ♀ ■ ▲ ♪ ☼ ♀ ☺ ♂ ▲ ─ ◀ ▼ ☺ ♀ ■ ▲ ♪

Which symbol is missing from the above sequence and from where within the sequence is it missing?

a) ▶
b) ♪
c) ♀
d) ■
e) ☼

24. Work from letter to adjacent letter horizontally and vertically, but not diagonally to spell out a 12-letter word. You must find the starting point and provide the missing letter.

D	E	E	N
E	T	E	I
R	P	R	

25. What number should replace the question mark?

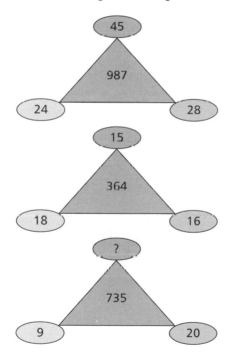

26.

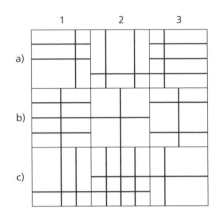

Looking at lines across and down, if the first two tiles are combined to produce the third tile, with the exception that like symbols are cancelled out, which of the above tiles is incorrect, and with which of the tiles below should it be replaced?

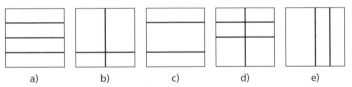

a)   b)   c)   d)   e)

27. Complete the equation by correctly identifying the missing part of the calculation from the list of options below.

$$\frac{36 + (9 \times 7)}{\sqrt{121}} = \frac{4 \times (?)}{5} - \frac{133}{7}$$

a) 6^2
b) $92 - 59$
c) 7×5
d) $3^3 + 9$

28. Which is the odd one out?
canticle, threnody, madrigal, libretto, aria

29. 2 3 6 5 9 2 7 4 8 3 1 9 7

Strike out all the odd numbers in the above list and multiply the remaining numbers together. Now take the total you have obtained and repeat the process, striking out any odd numbers, and multiplying the remaining numbers together.

What number are you left with?

30. Find two of the three words: that can be paired to form an anagram that is a synonym of the remaining word. For example, with LEG – MEEK – NET, the words LEG and NET form an anagram of GENTLE, which is a synonym of the remaining word, MEEK.

THIN – SUITCASE – KEEN

31. 349, (21), 763, (45), 299, (?)

What number should replace the question mark?

32. N 5 P D Q 7 3 4 T 8 F K Z L

Arrange the even numbers in descending order followed by the letters in forward alphabetical order followed by the odd numbers in ascending order.

33. ● — ● ● — ● ● ● — ○ — ○ ○ — ○ ○ ○ — ● — ●

Which two symbols continue the above sequence?

a) — ●
b) ● ●
c) ● —
d) — ○
e) ○ ●

34. Identify two words (one from each set of brackets) that form a connection (analogy), thereby relating to the words in capitals in the same way.

ABDUCTION   (winch, kidnap, ransom)
LARCENY   (theft, deceit, crime)

35. Each set of nine numbers relate to each other in a certain way. Work out the logic behind the numbers in the left-hand box in order to determine which number is missing from the right-hand box.

2	9	4		3	7	2
5	16	3		3	28	9
5	11	2		7	?	6

36. In the two numerical sequences below, one number that appears in the top sequence should appear in the bottom sequence and vice versa. Which two numbers should be changed round?

    100, 99, 97, 96, 94, 92

    100, 98, 97, 95, 94, 93

37. Select two words that are synonyms, plus an antonym of these two synonyms, from the list of words below.

    amass, accuse, question, cite, empower, absolve, forsake

38. How tall is a sapling that is six feet shorter than a wall that is seven times higher than the sapling?

39. Change one letter only in each word below to form a familiar phrase.

    IS WOOD NICE

40.

Which circle should replace the question mark?

  a)   b)   c)   d)   e)

Test Three

1. You are looking for one word in this paragraph. The word appears only once, its first letter is the ninth letter to appear after a certain vowel and the same vowel is the fifth letter to appear after its last letter.

2. Find the starting point and track from letter to letter along the lines to spell out the name of an American city (12 letters).

   There is one double letter in the name.

   Note: when travelling from letter to letter along a side of the triangle, lines may have to pass through letters that are not part of the solution.

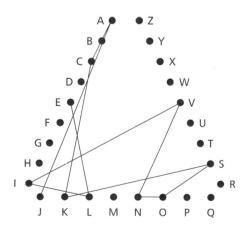

3. Sequence

Which option below continues the above sequence?

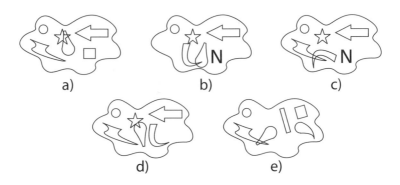

4. What numbers should replace the question marks?

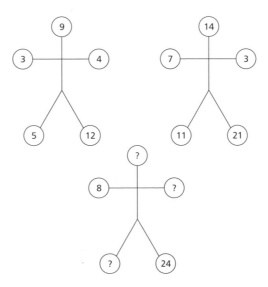

5. Taking the respective numerical position of the alphabet, decode the following phrase, for example IQ TEST = 9, 17, 20, 5, 19, 20 or 9172051920.

   121124121147192514 5

6. Solve each anagram to find two phrases that are spelt differently but sound alike, as in: 'a name', 'an aim'.

   SEMI ARC   CRIME ACE

7. Which number is the odd one out?

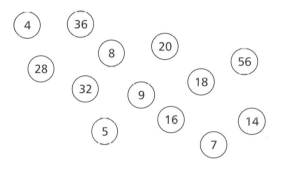

8. What phrase can be inserted into the bottom row to complete the three-letter words reading downwards?

   Clue: musical solo

A	F	H	D	L	P	H	P	M	W
G	A	U	I	E	A	O	E	A	A

9. Solve the cryptic clue below. The answer is a 10-letter word anagram contained within the clue.

> NEEDLEWORK
> DECORATES
> MY DIRE
> ROBE

10. What is a BURGEE a type of?

   a) elastic
   b) flag
   c) rope
   d) window
   e) food

11. Odd one out

Which is the odd one out?

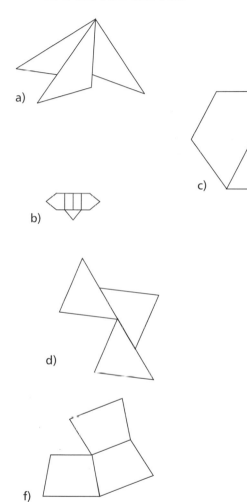

a)

b)

c)

d)

e)

f)

g)

12. Which two of these words are closest in meaning?

    GLUT, SUPPLICATION, AID, CACHE, GUIDANCE, PLEA

13. Which number comes next in this sequence?

    1, 2, 0, 3, −1, 4, ?

14. Complete each seven-letter word in such a way that the name of a novel is spelt out by the three letters inserted in each word. You are actually looking for six three-letter words.

    HO . . . AD
    SC . . . ED
    RO . . . CE
    SL . . . ER
    DI . . . RY
    RO . . . TE

15. What, with reference to this question, is the next number in the sequence below?

    3, 3, 5, 1, 3, 4, 1, 2, 3, 4, 1, 2, ?

16. Sequence

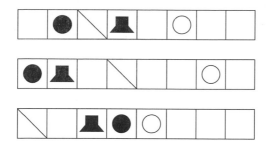

Which option below continues the above sequence?

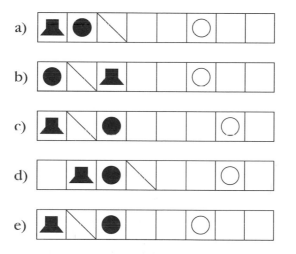

17. LOB is to ORE
    as ORB is to ?

18.

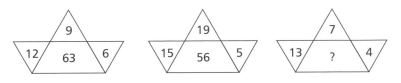

What number should replace the question mark?

19. Which two words that sound alike, but are spelt differently, mean:

SLACK/REQUIRES

20. Which word in brackets is opposite in meaning to the word in capitals?

FREQUENT (glow, restrain, avoid, discard, resort)

21. Each set of nine numbers relate to each other in a certain way. Work out the logic behind the numbers in the left-hand box in order to determine which number is missing from the right-hand box.

5	7	4		9	2	5
8	2	6		3	?	3
3	7	6		4	4	8

22. Select two words that are synonyms, plus an antonym of these two synonyms, from the list of words below.

thoughtful, pleased, uncouth, churlish, stubborn, lugubrious, rueful

23. How old is Jane if in eight years' time she will be twice as old as she was twenty years ago?

24. Identify two words (one from each set of brackets) that form a connection (analogy), thereby relating to the words in capitals in the same way.

    VITREOUS (glass, metal, brittle)
    CRYSTALLINE (opaque, granite, substance)

25. Which is the odd one out?
    a) | | e £ ℓ ▲ → ☺ ← © &
    b) ▲ ℓ ← ☺ → e Җ £ ¢ ¤ &
    c) £ ¢ Җ ℓ ® & → ☺ ← ▲
    d) e ¢ © ∏ £ § → ☺ ← ℓ
    e) ® £ & → ☺ ← e ∏ ¤ ©

26. Which number is the odd one out?
    3785   1563   2674   5967   4896

27. Use all the letters of the phrase TENDERLY SUITABLE LADY once each only to spell out three kinds of song.

28. Insert the numbers listed into the circles so that – for any particular circle – the sum of the numbers in the circles connected to it equals the value corresponding to that circled number in the list.

For example:

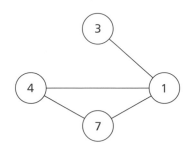

$1 = 14 (4 + 7 + 3)$
$3 = 1$
$4 = 8 (1 + 7)$
$7 = 5 (1 + 4)$

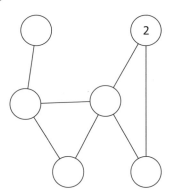

$1 = 13$
$2 = 8$
$3 = 14$
$4 = 1$
$5 = 5$
$6 = 4$

29. What letter is immediately to the left of the letter which is immediately below the letter which is two to the left of the letter N?

A	B	C	D	E	
F	G	H	I	J	
K	L	M	N	O	
P	Q	R	S	T	
U	V	W	X	Y	Z

30. & $ # & # $ # $ & # & $ $ # &

Which three symbols complete the above sequence?

a) & # $

b) $ & #

c) & $ #

d) $ # &

c) # $ &

31.

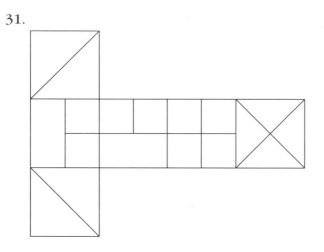

When the above is folded to form a cube, just one of the following can be produced. Which one?

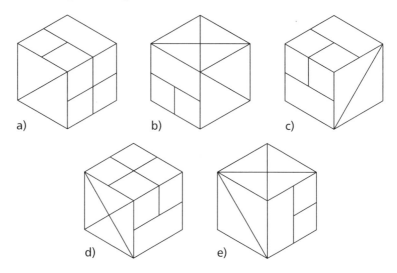

32. If seven men can build a house in 30 days, how long will it take 5 men to build the same house providing they all work at the same rate?

33. Complete the two eight-letter words reading clockwise
which must be opposite in meaning.
In each word you must find the starting point and
provide the two missing letters.

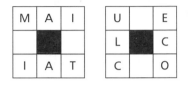

34. Complete the equation by correctly identifying the
missing part of the calculation from the list of options
below.

$$\frac{68 \times ?}{12} = \frac{\sqrt{1156}}{\sqrt{4}}$$

a) $\dfrac{24}{6}$

b) 1.2×3

c) $\sqrt{9}$

d) $10.5 - 2^2$

35. Which is the odd one out?
academy, presbytery, conservatory, seminary, university

36. What is the longest word in the English language that can
be produced from the letters below? No letter may be
used more than once.
M E P O C U W T L I

37. In the two numerical sequences below, one number that
appears in the top sequence should appear in the bottom
sequence and vice versa. Which two numbers should be
changed round?

15, 19, 27, 32, 39, 43, 51
12, 20, 24, 31, 36, 44, 48

38. What number should replace the question mark?

6	11		9	13		7	4
3	8		?	6		12	9

39. Each nine-letter word square is an anagram of a nine-letter word. Find the two words which are similar in meaning.

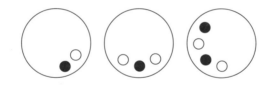

40.

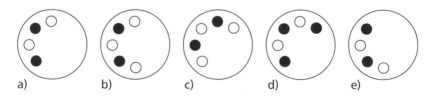

What comes next?

a)   b)   c)   d)   e)

Test Four

1. Which is the odd one out?

    CLAVICHORD, SPINET, HARPSICHORD, CLARION,
    ACCORDION

2. 'SLOW OR FAST ROADS' is an anagram of which familiar
    phrase: 2, 1, 4, 3, 5, which means the opposite of
    verbose?

3. 2586321 is to 2682
    as 94783219647 is to ?

4. What do the following have in common?

    RHAPSODY IN BLUE
    QUICK ON THE DRAW
    BOXING MATCHES
    WHISKY GALORE
    VENUS FLYTRAP
    QUESTION MARK
    PANTY GIRDLES

5. Shields

Which shield should replace the question mark?

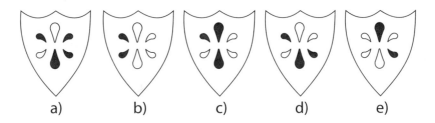

a)   b)   c)   d)   e)

6. Spiral clockwise round one of the circles and anti-
    clockwise round the other to find two words that have
    similar meanings.

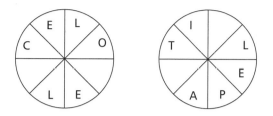

7. LATTICE : WINDOW

    Which two words below have the same relationship as the
    two words above?

    a) portal : gable
    b) embrasure : chimney
    c) mansard : roof
    d) parapet : door
    e) fascia : floor

8. Which word in brackets means the same as the word in
    capitals?

    INDISCRETION (crudity, sloth, folly, aversion, vacillation)

9. What numbers should replace the question marks?

7	5	4	6
5	8	10	8
6	?	?	7
8	6	7	9

10. What do the following words have in common?

PRECIOUS, CIRCLE, TONE, AUTOMATIC

11. A well-known phrase has had all its vowels removed and has been split into groups of three letters, which are in the correct order. What is the phrase?

KPT HBL LRL LNG

12. What is the missing number?

2	7	6	8	4
1	2	1	9	6
2	5	4	7	8
6	5	3	5	?

13. What comes next?

A, 1A, 111A, 311A, ?

14. Complete two magic word squares where the same four words in each square can be read both vertically and horizontally. Clues are given, but in no particular order.

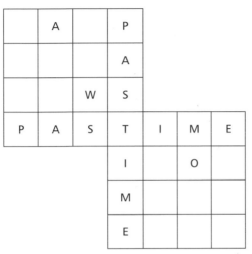

Clues:
1. Dense plant
2. Yard or street
3. Stretch of land
4. Moist
5. Someone in addition
6. Figure of worship

15. Comparison

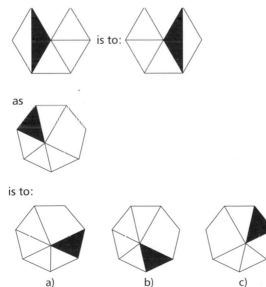

is to:

as

is to:

a)   b)   c)

16. Which is the odd one out?

    SALIFEROUS, EVACUATION, REGULATION,
    EXHAUSTION, INOCULATED, DUODECIMAL

17. Which number is the odd one out?

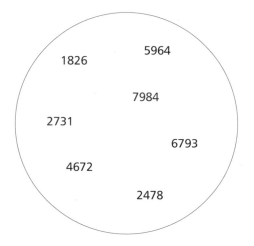

18. Which two words are most opposite in meaning?

    MALICIOUS, KNAVISH, HOPEFUL, SERVILE, PRINCIPLED,
    AWKWARD

19. Which other 12-letter weather word can be placed in the right-hand column in order to complete the three-letter words reading across?

H	A	
I	■	
G	■	
H	E	
P	A	
R	U	
E	A	
S	■	
S	I	
U	■	
R	■	
E	L	

20. I strode to Dorset, ate milk and rice in Limerick and bought Edna a beer in Aberdeen. Whom did I meet in Antrim?

21. A photograph measuring 7.5 cm by 3.25 cm is to be enlarged.
    If the enlargement of the longest side is 10.5 cm, what is the length of the shortest side?

22. Identify two words (one from each set of brackets) that form a connection (analogy), thereby relating to the words in capitals in the same way.
    SPHEROIDAL (rounded, angular, ellipse)
    ANNULAR (eclipse, ring, dome)

23. Complete the equation by correctly identifying the missing part of the calculation from the list of options below.
    $(4.25 + 2.75)^2 + ? = 5^3 - (9 \times 8)$
    a) 3
    b) 4
    c) 5
    d) 6

24. Only one group of six letters below can be arranged to spell out a six-letter word in the English language. Find the word.
    MUTLNO
    ABOFIG
    ANEDIT
    CIMOLU
    LOAWPC
    KNAURL
    ALCNOT

25. What number should replace the question mark?

6	8	6	3
5	2	5	7
9	5	9	?

26. The phrase FIX RELIEF OIL is an anagram of which saying (6, 2, 4).
    Clue: panacea

27. Which is the odd one out?
    acquit, exculpate, condone, absolve, vindicate

28. Which two symbols are missing from the sequence below and from where within the sequence are they missing?

■ ■ ▶ ■ ■ ■ ▲ ■ ■ ▼ ■ ■ ■ ◀ ■ ■ ▶ ■ ■ ■ ▲ ■ ■ ▼ ■ ■ ■ ◀ ■ ■
■ ▶ ■ ■ ■ ▲ ■ ■ ▼ ■ ■ ■ ◀ ■ ■ ▶ ■ ■ ■ ▲ ■ ■ ■ ■ ◀ ■ ■ ▶ ■
■ ■ ▲ ■ ■ ▼ ■ ■ ■ ◀ ■ ■ ▶ ■ ■ ■ ▲ ■ ■ ▼ ■ ■ ■ ◀ ■ ■ ▶ ■ ■
■ ▲ ■ ■ ▼ ■ ■ ■ ◀

a) ■ ▼
b) ◀ ■
c) ■ ■
d) ■ ▶
e) ■ ▲

29. In the two numerical sequences below, one number that appears in the top sequence should appear in the bottom sequence and vice versa. Which two numbers should be changed round?

3, 6, 18, 36, 108, 216, 432
2, 6, 12, 36, 72, 216, 648

30. What is the longest word in the English language that can be produced from the letters below? No letter may be used more than once.

    M Y U F L D G A K I

31. The top set of six numbers has a relationship to the set of six numbers below. The two sets of six boxes on the left have the same relationship as the two sets of six boxes on the right.

6	7	5	2	4	8		15	9	16	10	11	3
5	8	6	1	3	7		?	?	?	?	?	?

Which set of numbers should, therefore, replace the question marks?

a)

16	10	15	9	12	4

b)

7	9	14	18	7	2

c)

14	8	17	11	10	2

d)

13	10	15	7	9	5

e)

11	9	19	17	12	4

32. Draw the contents of the middle tile in accordance with the rules of logic already established.

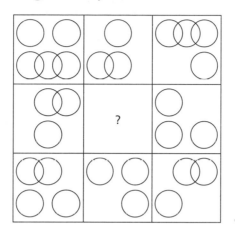

33. Find the starting point and work from letter to letter along the connecting lines to spell out a 14-letter word.

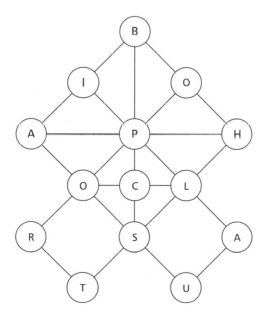

34. Which is the missing section?

2	3	5	6
7	?	?	11
15	?	18	19
20	21	23	24

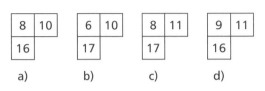

8	10
16	

a)

6	10
17	

b)

8	11
17	

c)

9	11
16	

d)

35. N 8 A K Z P E 6 5 G U M 3

Arrange the vowels in forward alphabetical order followed by the numbers in descending order followed by the consonants in reverse alphabetical order.

36. If A = 7, B = 4, C = 2, D = 9 and E = 3 calculate:

$$\frac{(A \times B) + (B \times C)}{\sqrt[3]{(D \times E)}}$$

37. Select two words that are synonyms, plus an antonym of these two synonyms, from the list of words below.

surplus, fervour, hunger, glut, mirth, paucity, joy

38. Which symbol continues the sequence below?

Ω Σ Ψ ♂ ♥ ♫ ☺ ‡ Ω Σ Ψ ♂ ♥ ♫ ☺ ‡ Ω Σ Ψ ♂ ♥ ♫ ☺

a) ‡

b) ♫

c) Σ

d) ‡

e) Σ

39. Harry, Larry and Carrie share out a certain sum of money between them. Harry gets 35%, Larry gets 3/5 and Carrie gets £125.

How much is the original sum of money?

40. Which is the missing section?

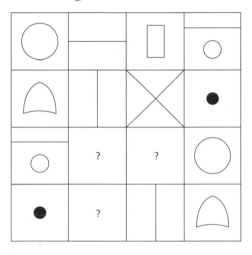

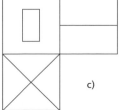 a)

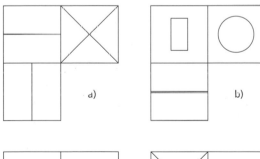 b)

c)

d)

Test Five

1. How many circles appear below?

2. Complete the six words so that two letters are common
    to each word. That is, reading across, the same two letters
    that end the first word also start the second word, etc.
    The two letters that end the sixth word are also the first
    two letters of the first word, to complete the circle.

    . . A B . .
    . . N G . .
    . . I E . .
    . . N D . .
    . . A C . .
    . . S S . .

3. You have accidentally left the plug out of the bath and are
    attempting to fill the bath with both taps full on. The hot
    tap takes three minutes to fill the bath and the cold tap two
    minutes, and the water empties through the plug hole in
    six minutes. In how many minutes will the bath be filled?

4. Sequence

    What continues the above sequence?

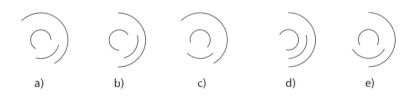

    a)   b)   c)   d)   e)

5. Which word is the odd one out?

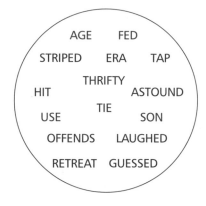

AGE   FED
STRIPED   ERA   TAP
THRIFTY
HIT   ASTOUND
TIE
USE   SON
OFFENDS   LAUGHED
RETREAT   GUESSED

6. What number should replace the question mark?

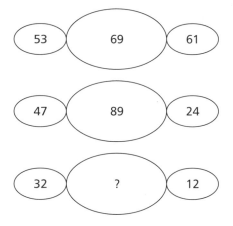

53   69   61

47   89   24

32   ?   12

7. What do these words have in common?

ABUNDANCE, ALLEVIATE, UNTRUTHS, PROCAINE,
CHAMBER

8. What letter should replace the question mark?

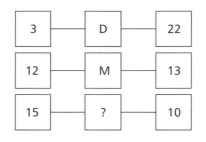

9. Solve the anagram in brackets to complete the quotation correctly. You are looking for a two-word answer (5, 6).

Clue: convenience

The (FUTILE SLOTH) is the basis of western civilization (Alan Coult).

10. Sequence

What comes next in the above sequence?

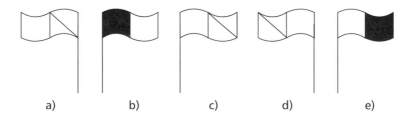

11. Insert the numbers 1–5 in the circles so that for any particular circle the sum of numbers in the circles connected directly to it equals the value corresponding to the number in that circle, as given in the list.

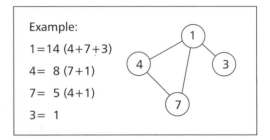

Example:

1 = 14 (4+7+3)

4 = 8 (7+1)

7 = 5 (4+1)

3 = 1

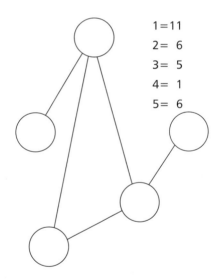

1 = 11

2 = 6

3 = 5

4 = 1

5 = 6

12. Pick a letter from each circle and, reading anti-clockwise, spell out two words that are synonyms. Each word starts in a different circle.

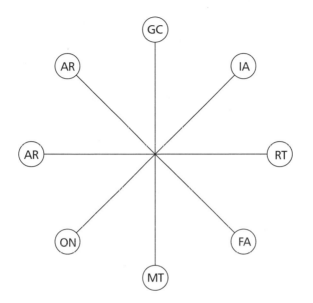

13. Create two words using the following 10 letters each once only:

    Clue: easier tariff

    MXERPLAITS

14. MUSIC: COMPOSE
    DEVICE: a) use
              b) create
              c) construct
              d) invent
              e) change

15. Find two of the three words that will form an anagram synonymous with the word remaining.

    Example: LEG – MEEK – NET = MEEK – GENTLE (LEG, NET)

    TRUCE – NONE – MEET

16. What number continues this sequence?

    987, 251, 369, 872, 513, ?

17. Move horizontally and vertically, but not diagonally, to spell out a 12-letter word. You must provide the missing letters.

E	F	O	
S	O	N	P
	I	A	L

18. What comes next in this sequence?

    7, 8, 9, 10, 12, 14, 16, 20, 21, 28, ?

19. Which two words are closest in meaning?

    EXPLORER, VAGRANT, MINSTREL, RESIDENT, SOLDIER, ITINERANT

20. Change one letter only from each word to find a familiar phrase:

    OUT OF IRE

21. Which number is the odd one out?
    17458, 13762, 13545, 29498, 27993

22. Complete the six-letter words below so that the same two
    letters that finish the first word start the second word, the
    same two letters that finish the second word start the
    third word etc. The same two letters that finish the eighth
    word also start the first word to complete the circle.

    * * N A * *
    * * M P * *
    * * G A * *
    C * M B * *
    * * L E * *
    * * N I A *
    * * L U * *
    * E F U * *

23. 6 3 7 3 6 9 2 4 8 7 3 9 1 6 8 2 9 7 4 1
    What is the sum of all the odd numbers that are immedi-
    ately followed by an even number in the above list?

24. In the two numerical sequences below, one number that
    appears in the top sequence should appear in the bottom
    sequence and vice versa. Which two numbers should be
    changed round?

    15, 18, 24, 34, 45, 60
    12, 16, 21, 27, 33, 42

25. Identify two words (one from each set of brackets) that
    form a connection (analogy), thereby relating to the
    words in capitals in the same way.

    CAUSTIC (dogmatic, sad, bitter)
    FACILE (effortless, impatient, confused)

26. A market stall owner took delivery of a consignment of eggs and to his chagrin found that a number were cracked. On counting them up he found that 62 were cracked which was 4% of the total consignment.

How many eggs were in the consignment?

27. Complete the equation by correctly identifying the missing part of the calculation from the list of options below.

$$\frac{\sqrt{(51 + 22 + 8)}}{?} = \frac{4^3 + 5}{\sqrt{529}}$$

a) $\sqrt{16} \times 3$
b) 3^2
c) 10
d) 3

28. Which of the following is not an anagram of a member of the reptile family?

AT GORILLA

BETTER RAVE

CLEAN HOME

COOL CIDER

SKI BAILS

29. Select two words that are synonyms, plus an antonym of these two synonyms, from the list of words below.

obscene, weak, exigent, omnipotent, venerable, supreme, painful

30. Which is the missing section?

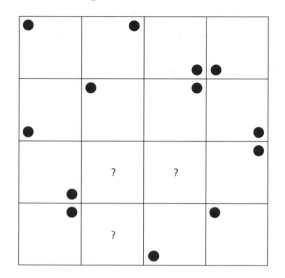

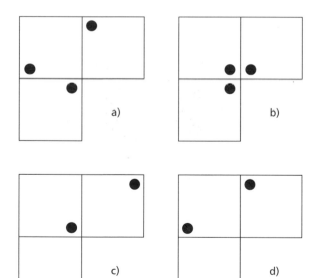

31. Which symbol is missing from the sequence below and from where within the sequence is it missing?

    ← ← → ↓ ↕ ↕ ↔ → ↑ ← ← → ↕ ← ← → ↓ ↕ ↕ ↔ → ↑ ← ←
    → ↕ ← ← → ↓ ↕ ↔ → ↑ ← ← → ↕ ← ← → ↓ ↕ ↕ ↔ → ↑ ←
    ← → ↕ ← ← → ↓ ↕ ↕ ↔ → ↑ ← ← → ↕

    a) ↑
    b) ↕
    c) ←
    d) ↓
    e) ↔

32. What number should replace the question mark?
    1, 8, 10, 19, 26, 28, 37, 44, ?

33. Place a word in the brackets that means the same as the definitions outside the brackets.

    backfire   (   )   narrative

34. What number should replace the question mark?

6	8		9	7		5	9
4	8		6	3		4	?

35. What letter comes midway between the letter two below the letter D and the letter four to the left of the letter Z?

A	B	C	D	E	
F	G	H	I	J	
K	L	M	N	O	
P	Q	R	S	T	
U	V	W	X	Y	Z

36. Draw the contents of the middle tile in accordance with the rules of logic already established.

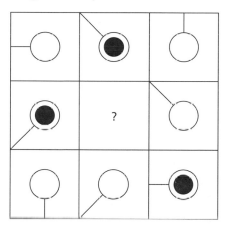

37. Which is the odd one out?

a) # $ % & ?

b) @ $ # % &

c) ▼ ■ ◄ ▲ —

d) ■ ▲ ◄ — ▼

e) # % ? $ &

38. The top set of six numbers has a relationship to the set of six numbers below. The two sets of six boxes on the left have the same relationship as the two sets of six boxes on the right.

9	2	6	3	7	5		4	2	8	11	4	7
9	11	17	20	27	32		?	?	?	?	?	?

Which set of numbers should, therefore, replace the question marks?

a)

4	7	15	24	28	32

b)

9	11	19	30	34	41

c)

4	6	14	25	29	36

d)

9	15	18	22	31	42

e)

4	6	15	26	31	38

39. Arrange the letters in reverse alphabetical order, followed by the odd numbers in descending order followed by the even numbers in ascending order.

P 5 9 K S 8 T F L 6 2 M

40. Complete the two eight-letter words reading clockwise which must be similar in meaning.
In each word you must find the starting point and provide the two missing letters.

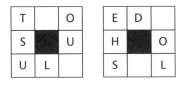

Test Six

1. Pair a word in list A with its related adjective in list B.

List A	List B
FLUVIAL	ROOK
VERNAL	PARROT
PSITTACINE	RIVER
CORVID	SPRING

2. What number should replace the question mark?

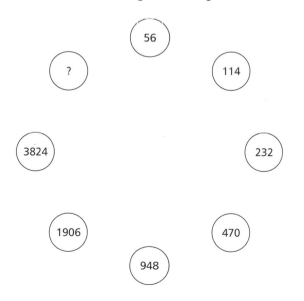

3. Comparison

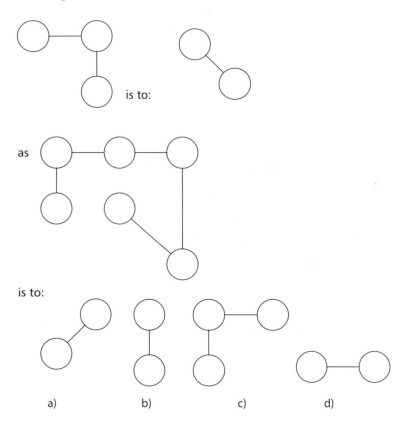

a)   b)   c)   d)

4.   63 : 369
     47 : 7411
     86 : ?

5.   Add one letter, not necessarily the same letter, to each
     word at the front, end or middle to find two words that
     are synonyms.

     RUSH, BEAK

6. Start at one of the corner squares and spiral clockwise round the perimeter to spell out a nine-letter word and finish at the centre square. You must provide the missing letters.

R	E	
A	R	
C	E	K

7. Which number comes next in the following sequence?

53472, 2435, 342, ?

8. Which of the following is not an anagram of an animal?

BRISK PONG
PUNCH KIM
RED OPAL
MOMS HOUR
FAB FOUL

9. What letter completes this sequence?

A B D O P Q ?

10. Which word in brackets means the same as the word in capitals?

PROGENY (skill, lineage, movement, progress, vocation)

11. Which three words can be inserted so that the phrase is palindromic, ie it reads the same backwards and forwards?

    A DOG! . . . . A PAGODA

12. How many lines appear below?

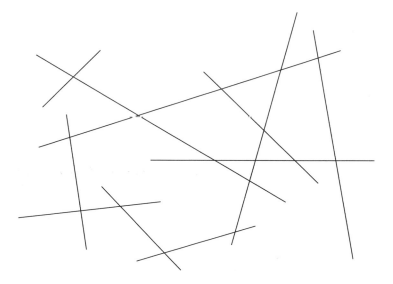

13. Sequence

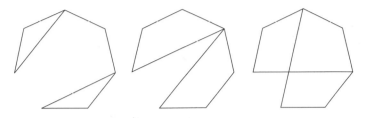

What comes next in the above sequence?

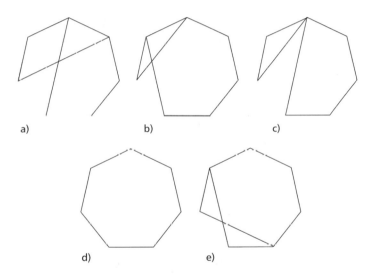

14. Below are eight CARING words. Take one letter from each of the eight words in turn to spell out a ninth CARING word.

Clue: dependable

FERVENT, CORDIAL, DOTING, DEVOTED, ATTACHED, FOND, AMOROUS, LOVING

15.

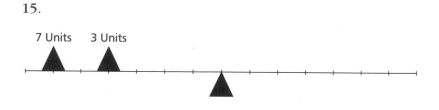

You have a range of weights available from 1–10 units. They are all single weights. Which one should you use to balance the scale, and where should you place it?

16. OLD ELASTIC is an anagram of which 10-letter word?

17. Odd one out

Which is the odd one out?

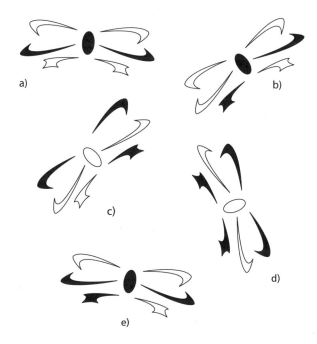

18. Find the phrase that has been hidden by removing the initial letter of each word, then removing the space between them.

    NHEEVEL

19. What number should replace the question mark?

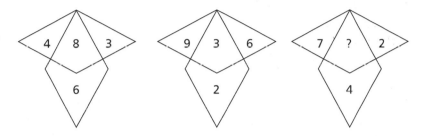

20. PERIGEE :   APOGEE
    PERIHELION : a) azimuth
                  b) eliptic
                  c) orrery
                  d) nadir
                  e) aphelion

21. What number should replace the question mark?

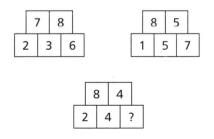

22. Change the position of four words only in the paragraph below so that it then makes perfect sense.

    Clandestine detection of vital information that cannot be obtained by any required means requires the recruitment of agents who are able to obtain the overt intelligence without collection.

23. Arrange the odd numbers in descending order followed by the letters in forward alphabetical order followed by the even numbers in ascending order.

    4 N T 8 5 B Z 2 9 K J 6 P

24. In the two numerical sequences below, one number that appears in the top sequence should appear in the bottom sequence and vice versa. Which two numbers should be changed round?

    15, 30, 48, 63, 86, 96, 114

    20, 32, 47, 59, 74, 81, 101

25. Identify two words (one from each set of brackets) that form a connection (analogy), thereby relating to the words in capitals in the same way.

    PEDICEL (leaf, flower, stalk)

    PISTOL (blossom, stamen, flower)

26.

is to:

as:

is to:

a)   b)   c)   d)   e)

27. David and George had 170 between them; however, George had one and a half times as many as David.

How many did each have?

28. Select two words that are synonyms, plus an antonym of these two synonyms, from the list of words below.

    pleasant, successful, amiable, angry, trite, impolite, glib

29. Which is the odd one out?
    a) ¶ ® § ¥ £ ◄ ■
    b) ∑ ↕ ╫ ♫ ♣ ☺ ╟
    c) ◄ Ω ╫ ☺ ↔ Ψ ♫
    d) £ Ω ∑ ♠ Ψ ☺ ╫
    e) ¶ Ω Ψ ↔ ∏ Ω ■

30. Find two of the three words: that can be paired to form an anagram that is a synonym of the remaining word. For example, with LEG – MEEK – NET, the words LEG and NET form an anagram of GENTLE, which is a synonym of the remaining word, MEEK.

    HOP – LATER – SURFEIT

31. I travel to work each morning by train and bus and take the same journey home each evening.
    If each train journey takes 39 minutes and each bus journey takes 17 minutes longer, what is my total travelling time in hours and minutes in a five-day working week?

32.

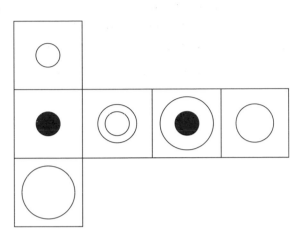

When the above is folded to form a cube, just one of the
following can be produced. Which one?

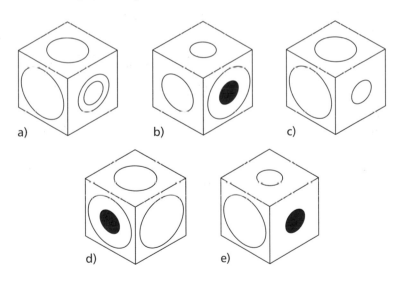

a) b) c)

d) e)

33. Which symbol is missing from the sequence below and from where within the sequence is it missing?

⌐⅃ ⅃ ╬╥╥⊣ ╠ ‖ ⊥ ┗ ⌐⅃ ⅃ ╬╥╥⊣ ╠ ‖ ⊥ ┗ ⌐⅃ ⅃ ╬╥╥⊣ ╠
‖ ⊥ ┗ ⌐⅃ ⅃ ╬╥╥⊣ ╠ ‖ ⊥ ┗ ⌐ ⅃ ╬╥╥⊣ ╠ ‖⊥ ┗ ⌐⅃ ⅃ ╬╥╥
⊣ ╠ ‖

a) ⅃

b) ‖

c) ⊥

d) ╠

e) ⅃

34. The top set of six numbers has a relationship to the set of six numbers below. The two sets of six boxes on the left have the same relationship as the two sets of six boxes on the right.

12	26	29	62	58	19		16	24	98	31	56	48
3	8	11	8	13	10		?	?	?	?	?	?

Which set of numbers should, therefore, replace the question marks?

a)

7	12	11	9	14	8

b)

16	13	19	4	10	18

c)

6	7	16	9	13	8

d)

7	6	17	4	11	12

e)

15	9	13	7	12	11

35. Find the starting point and work from letter to letter along the connecting lines to spell out a 10-letter word. You have to provide the missing letter.

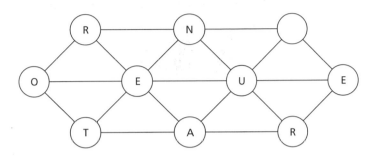

36. Add four consecutive letters of the alphabet, not necessarily in the same order, to complete the word below.

A * * I * A T *

37. Complete the equation by correctly identifying the missing part of the calculation from the list of options below.

$$125\% \times \frac{48}{\sqrt{256}} = 1.9 + ? + 1.5$$

a) 0.35
b) 0.45
c) 0.28
d) 0.4

38.   38629   is to   12
    and   14637   is to   11
    and   79652   is to   21
    therefore   52968   is to   ?

39. Which is the odd one out?
    denominator, aliquot, divisor, factor, integer

40. What number should replace the question mark?

Test Seven

1. Sequence

What comes next in the above sequence?

    a)   b)   c)   d)   e)

2. Which other sport-related phrase can be placed in the right-hand column reading downwards in order to complete the six three-letter words reading across? The phrase you are looking for has two words (8, 4).

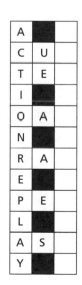

A		
C	U	
T	E	
I		
O	A	
N		
R	A	
E		
P	E	
L		
A	S	
Y		

3. Which word continues this sequence?

    COUNTERFEIT, FLOUNDERING, ENCOUNTERED,
    SUBJOINDERS

    Is it: viscountess, dumbfounded or preannounce?

4. What number should replace the question mark?

    Clue: think laterally

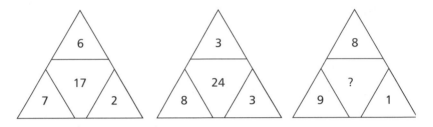

5. Which of the following is not an anagram of 'intelligence
    test'?

    TESTING ELECT LINE
    TESTING CLIENTELE
    TIES GENTLE CLIENT
    LET TESTING CLIENT
    GET LITTLE INCENSE
    ELICIT GENTLE NETS

6. Which of the numbers, from 1 to 121, appears in the grid twice, and which number is missing?

61	102	30	115	80	32	73	110	36	89	18
90	35	119	74	117	83	48	26	11	95	50
49	113	19	7	101	41	15	3	94	44	13
85	14	25	120	53	109	43	23	29	81	6
37	99	98	2	108	78	62	34	56	69	40
60	10	24	93	72	22	107	51	1	118	28
33	75	92	47	104	86	114	17	76	105	21
82	4	27	116	52	12	84	71	111	63	8
91	59	16	68	39	66	96	25	100	70	38
20	42	79	9	55	64	77	5	54	88	45
67	103	46	97	31	87	106	58	121	65	112

7. Which word in brackets is opposite in meaning to the word in capitals?

GRUESOME (enjoyable, appealing, wholesome, young, virtuous)

8. What number should replace the question mark?

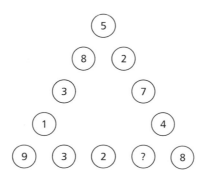

9. Solve the clues to find four six-letter words. The same three letters are represented by XYZ in each word.

X Y Z . . .   Clue: bovine animals
. X Y Z . .   Clue: attack with severe criticism
. . X Y Z .   Clue: find
. . . X Y Z   Clue: type of grape

10. Sequence

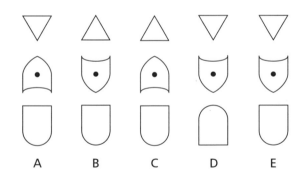

What comes next in the above sequence?

A   B   C   D   E

11. Change CAPRICORN to LIBRA. Each word repeats several letters from the word above it as indicated by *.

C A P R I C O R N
  * * * * * * .
. .   * * *   . .
  . .   * * *   .
      L I B R A

12. Find the starting point and follow the correct route from circle to circle to spell out a phrase (4, 2, 1, 3)

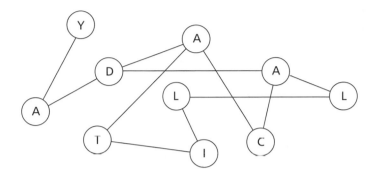

13. Insert a three-letter word that will complete the first word and start the second.

   SEA (. . .) NET

14. A number of antonyms of the keyword are shown. Take one letter from each of the antonyms, in order, to spell out another antonym of the keyword.

   KEYWORD : OMNIPOTENT

   ANTONYMS : INFERIOR, IMPOTENT, POWERLESS,
               VULNERABLE, FRAIL, INCAPABLE

15. SUNDAY
    MONDAY
    WEDNESDAY
    SATURDAY
    WEDNESDAY

   Which day comes next?

16. Sequence

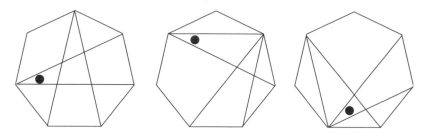

What comes next in the above sequence?

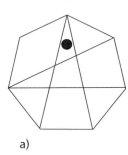

a)

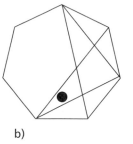

b)

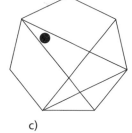

c)

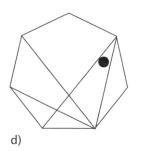

d)

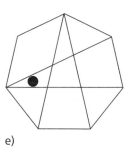

e)

17. Visit each square once only and finish at the centre square to collect the treasure. 1E means one square East, 2W means two squares West.

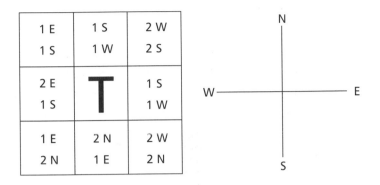

18. Solve each anagram to find two phrases that are spelt differently but sound alike, as in 'a name', 'an aim'.

    WOKEN CANON   INTO NOON

19. The grid contains 25 different letters of the alphabet. What is the longest word that can be found by starting anywhere and working from square to square horizontally, vertically and diagonally, and not repeating a letter?

    Clue: Significantly

Q	U	J	X	F
W	N	O	E	K
S	V	D	C	R
G	I	Y	A	H
P	M	L	B	T

20. What do the following have in common?

    TOTAL ECLIPSE
    A PIG IN A POKE
    WHITE ADMIRALS

21. Each set of nine numbers relate to each other in a certain way. Work out the logic behind the numbers in the left-hand box in order to determine which number is missing from the right-hand box.

3	7	11		1	5	9
7	5	3		8	?	4
2	6	10		5	9	13

22. Identify two words (one from each set of brackets) that form a connection (analogy), thereby relating to the words in capitals in the same way.

    ATOMISTIC   (elemental, part, essential)

    HOLISTIC   (whole, sacred, optional)

23. Which three symbols continues the sequence below?

    ⫪⫪⫫ ⌐ ⌐⌐ ⊦⊦⊣⫪⫪⫫ ⌐ ⌐⌐ ⊦⊦⊣⫪⫪⫫ ⌐

    a) ⌐⌐⌐
    b) ⌐ ⊦ ⌐
    c) ⊦⊣⫪
    d) ⌐⌐ ⊦
    e) ⫪ ⊦⫪

24. Mo has one and a quarter times as many as Joe and Flo has one and a quarter times as many as Mo. Altogether they have 61.
How many has each?

25. Which is the odd one out?
honey, saccharin, saffron, sugar, syrup

26. Which two circles come next?

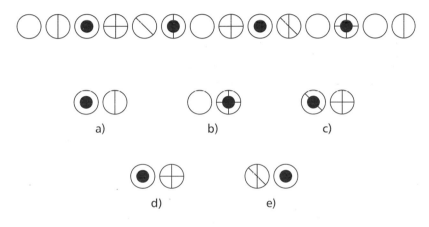

a)   b)   c)

d)   e)

27. In the two numerical sequences below, one number that appears in the top sequence should appear in the bottom sequence and vice versa. Which two numbers should be changed round?
10, 23, 37, 55, 74, 95
12, 23, 38, 54, 74, 97

28. What number should replace the question mark?

364	(7284)	276
423	(2475)	535
617	(?)	382

29. Change the position of three words only in the paragraph below so that it then makes complete sense.

    A Dutch inventor Cornelius van Drebbel managed to build a type of submarine in 1620. He wrapped a wooden rowboat tightly in waterproof tubes and fused air floats with leather reaching to the surface to provide oxygen.

30. A farmer has 232 yards of fencing and wishes to enclose a rectangular area of the greatest possible area. What will be its area?

31. DIG DIVINE HEAVEN is an anagram of which two words which sound alike but are spelled differently and mean, respectively, *criticized something harshly* and *encroach upon.*

32. Complete the equation by correctly identifying the missing part of the calculation from the list of options below.

    $$(6.25 \times 7) \times 4 \quad = \quad \frac{525}{? - (0.75 \times 4)}$$

    a) 2.52

    b) $\dfrac{6}{1.5}$

    c) 2.5 × 2

    d) $\sqrt{36}$

33. Select two words that are synonyms, plus an antonym of these two synonyms, from the list of words below.

    trim, earthy, spruce, sluggish, bedraggled, genial, agile

34. Which is the odd one out?

 a) ☼ ♣ ♀ — ↕ ▲ =
 b) ▲ ↕ ♣ ♀ ☼ — =
 c) — ♣ ☼ ‖ ♀ ▲ =
 d) = ↕ ▲ ♀ ♣ — ☼
 e) ♣ ☼ ↕ = ▲ ♀ —

35. How many boxes do you require if you have to pack 270 pairs of shoes into boxes that each hold 36 shoes?

36. Which set of circles should replace the question marks?

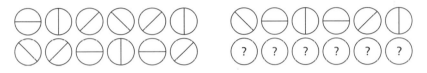

 a)
 b)
 c)
 d)
 e)

37. Arrange the even numbers in descending order followed by the odd numbers in ascending order followed by the letters in reverse alphabetical order.

 W T 8 K J 7 P R V N 6 2 5 D E S 9 3 F

38. What number should replace the question mark?

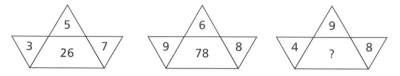

39. Find the starting point and work from letter to adjacent letter horizontally and vertically, but not diagonally to spell out a 12-letter word. You must provide the missing letter.

I		S	I
E	F	R	T
C	E	O	N

40. Complete the two eight-letter words reading clockwise which must be opposite in meaning.
In each word you must find the starting point and provide the two missing letters.

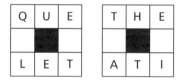

Test Eight

1. Only one set of letters below can be arranged into a five-letter word. Can you find the word?

    KIRCE
    EMRUD
    ONTDI
    ENCID

2. What number should replace the question mark?

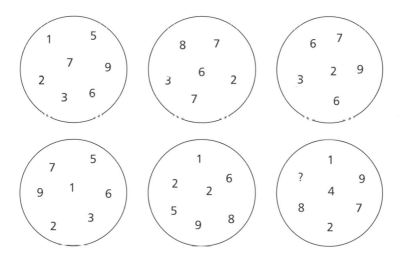

3. Solve the cryptic clue below. The answer is a nine-letter word anagram contained within the clue.

> INCLEMENT
> WEATHER
> SPOILT
> MINOR ARTS

4. What famous building can be inserted into the bottom line to complete nine three-letter words reading downwards?

T	O	W	E	R	O	F	L	O	N	D	O	N
	B	A	A		W	E	A			I	D	I

5. Comparison

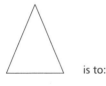 is to:

as

is to:

    a)   b)   c)   d)   e)

6. In a game of 10 players lasting for 30 minutes, five
    reserves substitute each player, so that all players,
    including reserves, are on the pitch for the same
    length of time. How long is each player on the pitch?

7.

25	13	10	1	17
8	24	11	12	4
19	6	21	7	5
9	15	5	18	3
14	20	22	16	2

What number is two places away from itself, plus 3, three
places away from itself doubled, two places away from
itself minus 2, two places away from itself plus 4, two
places away from itself minus 1, and two places away
from itself plus 6?

8. Start at one of the corner squares and spiral clockwise
    round the perimeter to spell out a nine-letter word,
    finishing at the centre square. You must provide the
    missing letters.

F	E	A
E	T	T
		I

9. Comparison

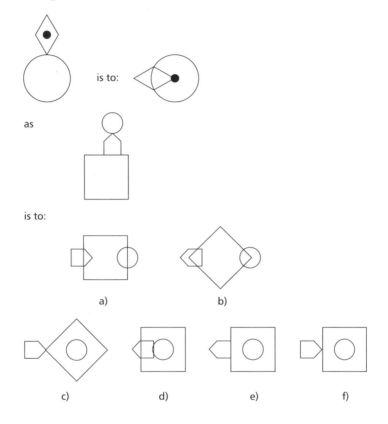

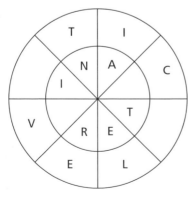

10.

Complete two words, one reading clockwise round the inner circle and one anti-clockwise round the outer circle. You must provide the missing letters. The two words are related in that they form a phrase.

11. Add one letter, not necessarily the same letter, to each word at the front, end or middle to find two words that are synonyms.

    COOK, HEAT

12. Which word in brackets is opposite in meaning to the word in capitals?

    SURREPTITIOUS   (servile, trusty, scarce, overt, unauthorized)

13. What number continues this sequence?

    1, 4, 8, 13, 19, ?

14. Solve the two anagrams below to create a familiar phrase.

    Clue: Low-cost curiosity

    . P . . . . F . .   ... R T . . . .
    ↑ FRY ONE PAN ↑   ↑ YOU HURT GHOST ↑

15. Which is the odd one out?

    MOGUL, SHANG, TANG, MING, HAN

16. GENEALOGY :   ANCESTRY
    ETYMOLOGY :   a) knowledge
                  b) insects
                  c) fossils
                  d) inscriptions
                  e) words

17. What number should replace the question mark?

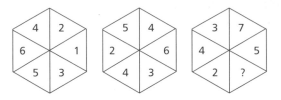

18. What three letters can be inserted into the brackets to spell out a girl's name when added to the first three letters and placed in front of the second three letters?

MAR (. . .) RON

19. Sequence

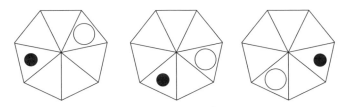

Which option below continues the above sequence?

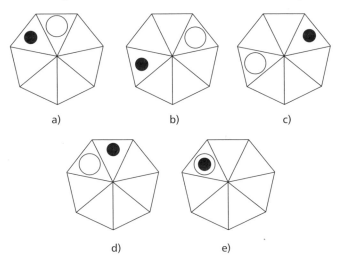

a) b) c)

d) e)

20. Odd one out

Which of these clock faces is the odd one out?

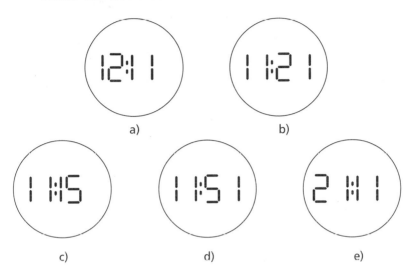

a)

b)

c)

d)

e)

21. What letter is two to the right of the letter which is two below the letter which comes midway between the letter immediately above the letter P and the letter immediately below the letter J?

A	B	C	D	E	
F	G	H	I	J	
K	L	M	N	O	
P	Q	R	S	T	
U	V	W	X	Y	Z

22. Which circle should replace the question mark?

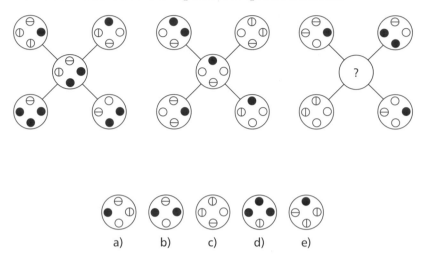

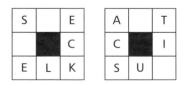

a)   b)   c)   d)   e)

23. In the two numerical sequences below, one number that appears in the top sequence should appear in the bottom sequence and vice versa. Which two numbers should be changed round?

2, 3, 5, 9, 18, 33

3, 4, 6, 10, 17, 34

24. Complete the two eight-letter words reading clockwise which must be opposite in meaning.
In each word you must find the starting point and provide the two missing letters.

S		E
	■	C
E	L	K

A		T
C	■	I
S	U	

25. Calculate the value of:

$$\frac{(277)^2}{554} \times 392$$

26. Identify two words (one from each set of brackets) that form a connection (analogy), thereby relating to the words in capitals in the same way.

    MOON (astral, satellite, lunar)

    STARS (solar, sidereal, celestial)

27. Which is the odd one out?
    a) & # • ▲ ¥ ¶ ¿ €
    b) Ж © £ ¢ ¤ § ®
    c) € ¿ ¶ ¥ ▲ • # &
    d) ▲ & ¢ § Ж © ¤
    e) ® § ¤ ¢ £ © Ж

28. What number should replace the question mark?
    19648, 1728, 112, ?

29. Combine four of the three-letter bits to find two words that are opposite in meaning.
    occ ity tan ver ult gle ard end can art

30. What number should replace the question mark?
    3529, 64, 9817, 115, 3257, ?

31.

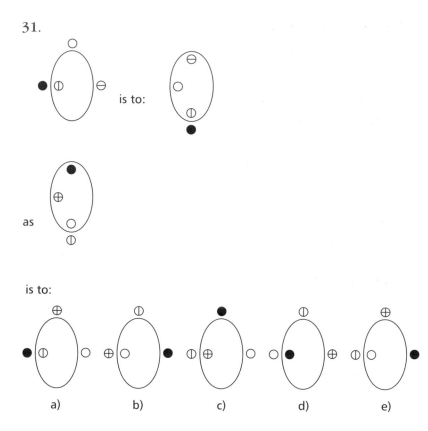

32. Which is the odd one out?
    circular, flyer, advertisement, stuffer, handbill

33. The average of three numbers is 26. The average of two of these numbers is 34. What is the third number?

34. Which three symbols continues the sequence below?

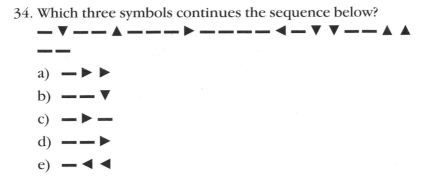

a) ━ ▶ ▶

b) ━━ ▼

c) ━ ▶ ━

d) ━━ ▶

e) ━ ◀ ◀

35. In the addition sum below only one of the decimal points is in the correct position. Alter four of the decimal points to make the sum correct.

23.57
2. 48
4 . 75
32 . 96
━━━━━
36 . 1507

36. Insert the numbers listed into the circles so that – for any
particular circle – the sum of the numbers in the circles
connected to it equals the value corresponding to that
circled number in the list.
For example:

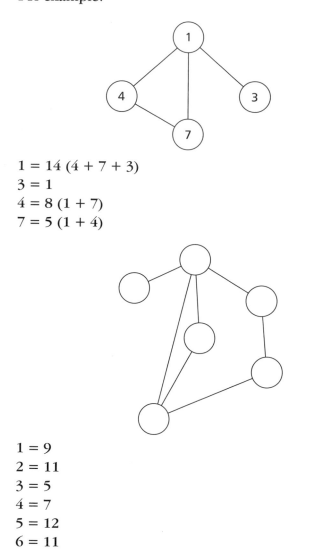

1 = 14 (4 + 7 + 3)
3 = 1
4 = 8 (1 + 7)
7 = 5 (1 + 4)

1 = 9
2 = 11
3 = 5
4 = 7
5 = 12
6 = 11

37. Select two words that are synonyms, plus an antonym of these two synonyms, from the list of words below.

    mimic, extol, carp, secure, reproach, apprehend, argue

38. Complete the equation by correctly identifying the missing part of the calculation from the list of options below.

    $$\frac{3^3 \div 2}{0.5^2} = \frac{6 \times 18}{(\,?\,) - 1.125}$$

    a) $\dfrac{(\,7\,)}{2}$

    b) $(2.5 \div 0.8)$

    c) (0.8×4)

    d) $(\sqrt{4} + 1.5)$

39. RIGHT, IT'S A START is an anagram of which two words meaning respectively *channel* and *direct* that sound alike but are spelled differently?

40. Each set of nine numbers relate to each other in a certain way. Work out the logic behind the numbers in the left-hand box in order to determine which number is missing from the right-hand box.

2	6	9		7	5	8
5	4	7		1	9	6
8	1	6		9	?	4

Test Nine

1.

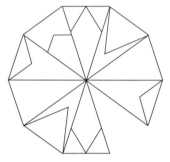

Find the missing section from the options below.

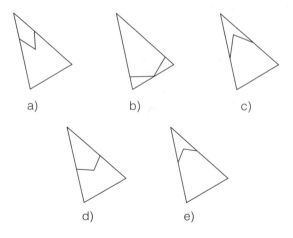

a)   b)   c)

d)   e)

2. Read clockwise to spell two antonyms by selecting one
    letter from each circle. Every letter is used and each word
    starts in a different circle.

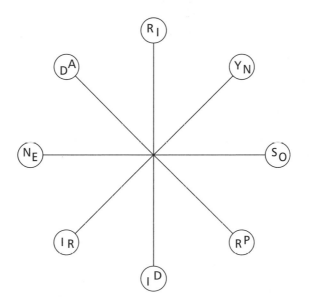

3. Which word in brackets means the same as the word in
    capitals?

    METAPHYSICAL (transient, esoteric, symbolic, planned,
    fastidious)

4.   Comparison

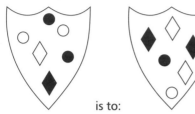

is to:

as

is to:

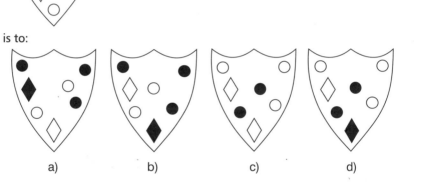

a)   b)   c)   d)

5.   What number should replace the question mark?

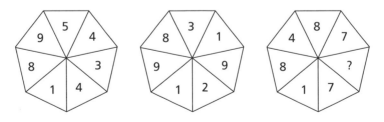

6. Solve each anagram to find two phrases that are spelt differently but sound alike, as in 'a name', 'an aim'.

   IMPEL UP   MY EEL PUP

7. What do these words have in common?

   PREFERABLE, PURVEYED, TARADIDDLE, BAGPIPES, BEJEWELLED

8. The words BEST and WORST are opposite in meaning. Find two more words that are opposite in meaning, one that must rhyme with BEST and one that must rhyme with WORST.

9. Odd one out

   Four of these pieces can be fitted together to form a perfect square. Which is the odd one out?

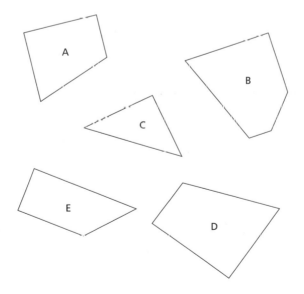

10. Missing tile

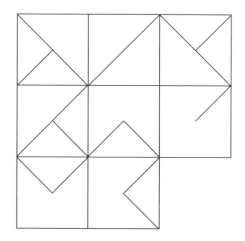

Choose the missing tile from the options below.

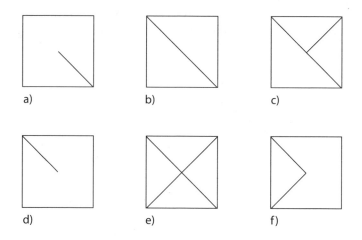

11. Which is the odd one out?

    Broth, elate, organ, glean, horse, idler, dance, eager, throb,
    groan, riled, angle, shore, caned, owned, agree, endow

12. SPIN   = 52
    LIST   = 51
    CALM   = 91
    LOAD   = 62
    LAND   = ?

13. What letter should replace the question mark?

?	E	D	D
A	S	A	E
N	A	L	R
S	N	D	S

14. Odd one out

Which is the odd one out?

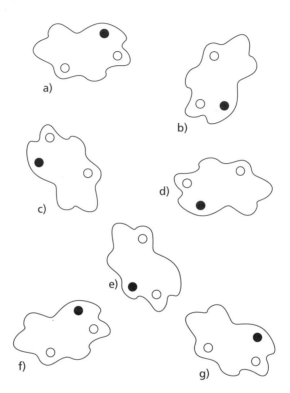

15. Read clockwise to find two eight-letter words that are antonyms. You have to find the starting point and provide the missing letters.

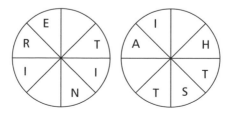

16. The phrase train-spotting (5–8) is an anagram of which other familiar phrase (8–5)?

    Clue: take the first step

17. A B C D E F G H

    What letter is two to the right of the letter immediately to the left of the letter that comes midway between the letter immediately to the left of the letter H and the letter two to the right of the letter A?

18. 7461 :   135

    6893 : a) 151
             b) 179
             c) 152
             d) 161
             e) 125

19. Insert the name of a fruit into the brackets reading downwards to complete the three-letter words.

    BI (.)
    LE (.)
    HA (.)
    HI (.)
    TO (.)
    FA (.)

20. What number should replace the question mark?

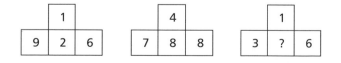

21. Select two words that are synonyms, plus an antonym of these two synonyms, from the list of words below.

extensive, spartan, slender, plush, expansive, ancient, palatial

22. Which two symbols continues the sequence below?

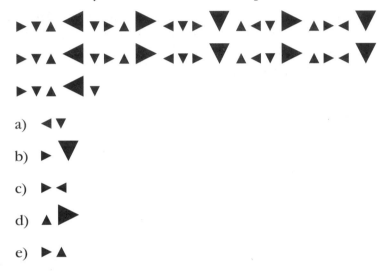

a) ◄▼

b) ► ▼

c) ►◄

d) ▲►

e) ►▲

23. DID TRUCE is an anagram of two 'this and that' words CUT, DRIED (cut and dried). GIRLY BATHER is an anagram of which two other this and that words?

24. In the two numerical sequences below, one number that appears in the top sequence should appear in the bottom sequence and vice versa. Which two numbers should be changed round?

100, 99, 97, 94, 88, 85

100, 98, 94, 90, 80, 70

25. Arrange the consonants in reverse alphabetical order followed by the odd numbers in ascending order followed by the vowels in reverse alphabetical order followed by the even numbers in descending order.

9 7 E G 6 T A F L P U 8 3 N Z K

26. Complete the equation by correctly identifying the missing part of the calculation from the list of options below.

$$\frac{5^2 \times 3}{\sqrt{225}} = \frac{1.25 \times 12}{? \times 24}$$

a) 1.5×4

b) 12.5%

c) $\dfrac{1}{6}$

d) 15%

27. Which is the odd one out?

a) N ♣ ☼ — ☺ — ☼ ♣ N

b) ♀ ♥ — ▲ — ♥ ♀

c) ╥ ╪ ‖ = ‖ ╪ ╥

d) ▲ = ‖ N ☼ N = ▲

e) ☼ ♣ — ♀ — ♣ ☼

28. What is the value of −16 − −25?

29.

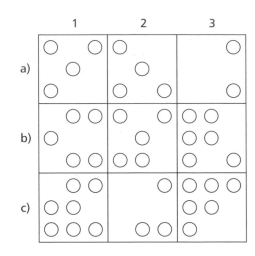

Looking at lines across and down, if the first two tiles are combined to produce the third tile, with the exception that like symbols are cancelled out, which of the above tiles is incorrect, and with which of the tiles below should it be replaced?

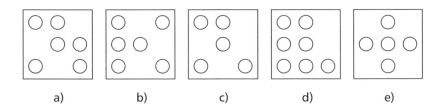

a)   b)   c)   d)   e)

30. Which is the odd one out?
   grapefruit, mandarin, lemon, apricot

31. The top set of six numbers has a relationship to the set of six numbers below. The two sets of six boxes on the left have the same relationship as the two sets of six boxes on the right.

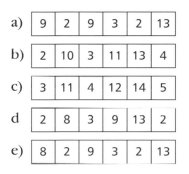

7	5	2	8	4	6		9	1	10	2	3	12
6	8	9	3	7	5		?	?	?	?	?	?

Which set of numbers should, therefore, replace the question marks?

a) | 9 | 2 | 9 | 3 | 2 | 13 |

b) | 2 | 10 | 3 | 11 | 13 | 4 |

c) | 3 | 11 | 4 | 12 | 14 | 5 |

d | 2 | 8 | 3 | 9 | 13 | 2 |

e) | 8 | 2 | 9 | 3 | 2 | 13 |

32. Combine three of the three-letter bits below to produce a word meaning SEARCH

ous   ten   nce   ghi   sua   out   wen   pit
pur   que

33. What is the length of the shortest side of a right-angled triangle if its two longest sides, one of which is the hypotenuse, are 28 and 35 units long?

34. What four-letter word can be inserted into each of the letter arrangements below to produce four words?

DEED   REEE   AMENT   IMIAL

35. What number should replace the question mark?

7, 22, 67, ? , 607

36. Which is the odd one out?

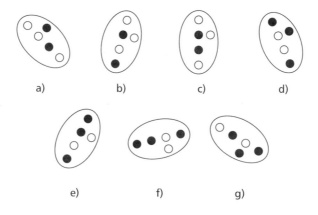

a) b) c) d)

e) f) g)

37. The new cost of an item which has been discounted by 15% is £32.30. What was the cost of the item originally?

38. Add the same letter four times to the group of letters below and then rearrange the 12 resultant letters to produce a 12-letter word.

A E E F G I O T

Clue: appliance

39. What number should replace the question mark?

758, 753, 748, 744, 740, 736, ?

40. Identify two words (one from each set of brackets) that form a connection (analogy), thereby relating to the words in capitals in the same way.

LONGING (past, contemplative, wistful)

CONCERN (share, solicitous, profound)

Test Ten

1. Which number is the odd one out?

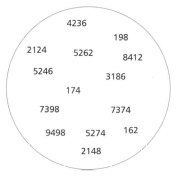

2. Spiral clockwise to find a 10-letter word. Only alternate letters are shown.

   Clue: outwit

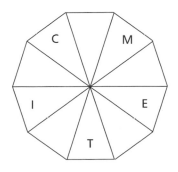

3. Comparison

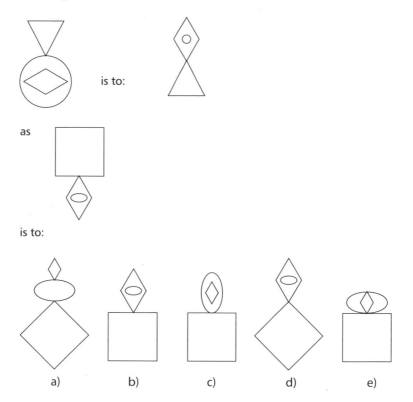

a)   b)   c)   d)   e)

4. Each square contains the letters of a nine-letter word. The two words are synonyms, and the overlapping letters T and A appear in each word. Can you unscramble them?

D	E	R		
E	C	T	M	E
I	A	A	L	I
		N	E	I

5. Find the starting point and track from letter to letter along the lines to spell out an item of jewellery (8, 4).

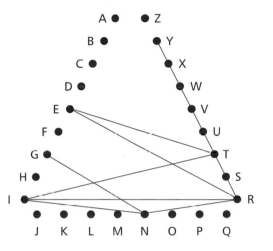

6. Squares

Which of the squares below has most in common with the square above?

a)   b)   c)   d)   e)

7. If presented with the words MAR, AM and FAR and asked to find the shortest word that contained all the letters from which these words could be produced, you should come up with the word FARM.

    Here is a further list of words:

    ANGRY, LYNCH, MAGIC

    What is the shortest English word from which all these words can be produced?

    Clue: captivatingly

8. Which box of numbers (A, B, C or D) should replace the box of question marks?

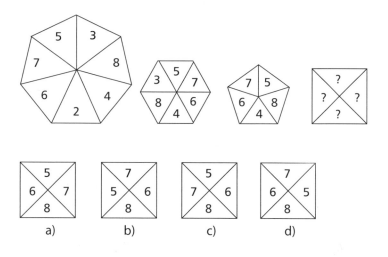

    a)   b)   c)   d)

9. Boxes

To which of the boxes below can a dot be added so that it meets the same conditions as in the box above?

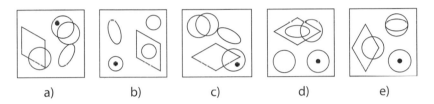

a)   b)   c)   d)   e)

10. What number should replace the question mark?

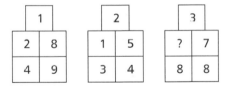

11. Read clockwise to find two words, one in each circle, that are antonyms. You must provide the missing letters.

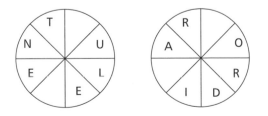

12. What number comes next in this sequence?

100, 99, 117, 108, ?

13. Comparison

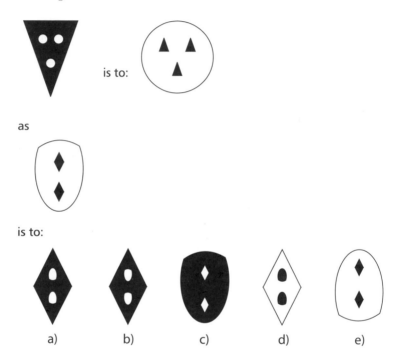

14. Read along the connecting lines from circle to circle to spell out a well-known phrase, especially at a certain time of the year (6, 4).

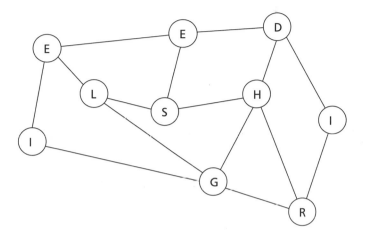

15. What word is both a weaving machine and means 'to menace'?

16. CRUSH VIOLA is an anagram of which 10-letter word?

17. Sequence

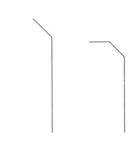

Which option below continues the above sequence?

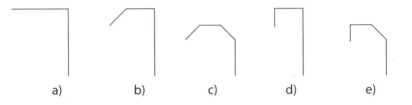

a)   b)   c)   d)   e)

18. What number comes next in this sequence?

1, 1.5, 2.5, 4, ?

19. Only one set of letters below can be arranged into a five-letter word. Can you find the word?

MUCHO
WINFO
ALPIC
DEPNU
BRENU

20. What word replaces the question marks in order to form seven five-letter words sandwiched between the letters on the right and the left?

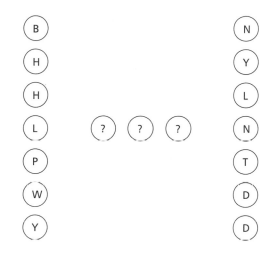

21. All the lines across have the same mathematical progression, and all the lines down have another mathematical progression. From the information already provided fill in all the remaining numbers.

		6			
		11			
				15	16
5	7				14
6			12	14	
		8	9		

22. Select two words that are synonyms, plus an antonym of these two synonyms, from the list of words below.

    inquisitive, cynical, caustic, sceptical, wise, confused, gullible

23. If meat in a river (3 in 6) is T(HAM)ES can you find a metallic element in the surrounding conditions (4 in 11)?

24.

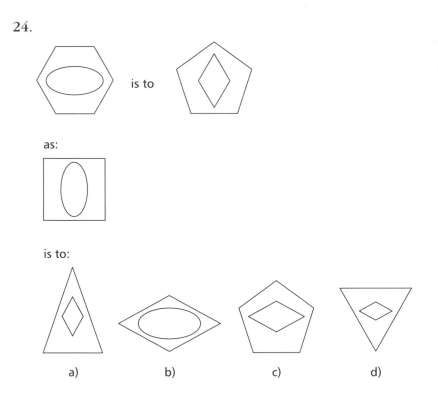

25. Which is the odd one out?
    pewter, invar, brass, steel, zinc

26. Identify two words (one from each set of brackets) that form a connection (analogy), thereby relating to the words in capitals in the same way.

    PERCOLATE   (drain, powder, filter)

    POACH   (simmer, liquid, steal)

27. Arrange the odd numbers in ascending order followed by the letters in reverse alphabetical order followed by the even numbers in descending order.

    K 3 T Z Y P E F L 7 2 X C 5 J 4

28. Which three symbols are missing from the sequence below and from where within the sequence are they missing?

    ☺ ♣ ♫ — ● — ♀ & ☺ ♣ ♫ — ● — ♀ & $ # @ ☺ ♣ ♫ — ●
    — ♀ & $ # @ ☺ ♣ ♫ — ● — ♀ & $ # @ ☺ ♣ ♫ — ● — ♀ &
    $ # @ ☺ ♣ ♫ — ● — ♀ & $ # @ ☺ ♣ ♫ — ● — ♀ & $ # @
    ☺ ♣ ♫ — ● — ♀ & $ # @ ☺ ♣ ♫ — ● — ♀

    a) — ♀ &
    b) $ # @
    c) ♫ — ●
    d) ☺ ♣ ♫
    e) # @ ☺

29. Which is the odd one out?
    abbreviated, clipped, transitory, fleeting, durable

30. In the two numerical sequences below, one number that appears in the top sequence should appear in the bottom sequence and vice versa. Which two numbers should be changed round?

    15, 37, 60, 84, 109, 131, 156

    18, 38, 62, 84, 110, 138, 168

31. Insert the same four-letter word into the letter arrangements below to produce two words.

    EL   ORNT

32. Which is the odd one out?

    dogmatic, catholic, illiberal, opinionated, petty

33. What number should replace the question mark?

    48 (68   )   64
    56 (73   )   24
    16 (?   )   32

34. Find five consecutive numbers in the list below that total 21.

    3 9 2 6 2 3 7 4 3 5 3 2 6 5 4 3 1 8 4 7 2

35. Combine three of the 3-letter bits below to produce a 9-letter word meaning a pedestrian walk.

    ine   lan   tie   out   ace   lor   ade   tin
    ewe   esp

36.

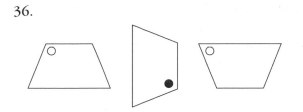

What comes next?

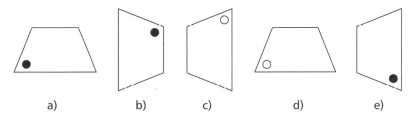

| a) | b) | c) | d) | e) |

37. Which three symbols continues the sequence below?

♂ ♂ ♠ ♠ ♪ ♫ ☺ ☺ ♂ ♂ ♠ ♠ ♪ ♫ ☺ ☺ ♂ ♂ ♠ ♠

a) ♫ ♫ ☺

b) ♪ ♪ ☺

c) ♪ ☺ ♫

d) ♪ ♫ ☺

e) ♫ ☺ ♪

38. Looking at straight lines horizontally, vertically or diagonally, what number is two places away from itself plus 2, three places away from itself multiplied by 2, three places away from itself divided by 2 and three places away from itself minus 2?

11	13	18	1	16
12	10	20	6	19
14	2	5	24	7
40	8	22	26	16
3	9	15	4	32

39. Complete the equation by correctly identifying the missing part of the calculation from the list of options below.

$$\frac{? - (6 \times 7)}{(\sqrt{64}) - 1} = \frac{75\% \, (12 \div 1.5)}{7.5 \div 2.5}$$

a) 64
b) (6 × 9)
c) 56
d) (131 – 73)

40. Each set of nine numbers relate to each other in a certain way. Work out the logic behind the numbers in the left-hand box in order to determine which number is missing from the right-hand box.

5	3	2		8	6	1
9	7	1		1	9	?
2	9	3		5	8	7

Test One

Answers

1. Vast melody

2. Fjord; it is a stretch of water. The others are all land

3. 6; $4 \times 9 = 36$

4. Reef; to spell out the numbers as follows:
   CART(ONE)NJOYMEN(TWO)RDSMI(THREE)F

5. E; a dot is only carried forward when it appears in the same position in two of the previous three circles

6. Talent

7. 27; add, then deduct, the sum of the digits of the previous number alternately each time, ie $36 - 3 - 6 = 27$

8. Delete; to give: fadc/desk, hole/lean, kite/tear

9. 48 mph
   Say, distance travelled = 60 miles each way

   therefore journey out = $\dfrac{60}{40} = 1.5$ hours

   journey in = $\dfrac{60}{60} = 1$ hour

   120 mile journey $= \dfrac{120}{2.5} = 48$ mph

10. Abundance

11. C; across

12. Double-page spread

13. A; the figure rotates into an upright position anti-clockwise. Black turns white and white turns black

14.

4	14	•15	1
9	•7	6	12
5	11	10	•8
•16	2	3	13

15. They all contain trees: le(gum)es, qu(ash)ed, af(fir)ms, cl(oak)ed

16. 51; $9 \times 5 = 45 + 6 = 51$

17. When prosperity comes, do not use all of it

18. Long, pithy

19. 0; looking down and across the sum of alternate numbers are equal, for example
$7 + 9 = 10 + 6$

20. Never look a gift horse in the mouth

21. p(lane)t

22. 56 and 54 should be swapped round
    The top sequence progresses +10, +11, +12, +13, +14
    The bottom sequence progresses +8, +10, +12, +14, +16

23. A; the symbols in the others all appear in the same order, albeit starting at a different symbol

24. F H K L N P 9 7 6 3 2

25. E; looking from top line to bottom line each pair of symbols swap round

26. Lock

27. E; multiply the odd numbers by 2 and divide the even numbers by 2

28. Diagonal, slanting

29. 156 lbs; 75% of 156 = 117. 39 × 4 = 156, 39 × 3 = 117

30. B

    ▶ ╬ ■ $ ⅃ & £ € ↕ Σ ▶ ╬ ■ $ ⅃ & £ € ↕ Σ ▶ ╬ ■ ($ ⅃ &) £ €
    ↕ Σ ▶ ╬ ■ $ ⅃ & £ € ↕ Σ ▶ ╬ ■ $ ⅃ & £ € ↕ Σ

31. 3; so that the sequence is palindromic (the numbers read the same backwards and forwards)

32. 1 in 56

$$\frac{3}{8} \times \frac{2}{7} \times \frac{1}{6} = \frac{6}{336} = \frac{1}{56}$$

33. Synonyms: vigilant, circumspect
    Antonym: remiss

34. A

35. And then some

36. B; the right half of the matrix is a mirror image of the left
    half

37. Cut, drill

38. 33 minutes: 12 noon less 33 minutes = 11.27
    11.27 less 48 minutes = 10.39
    9 am plus 99 minutes (3 × 33) = 10.39

39. Q

40. Turtle: each word can be suffixed by NECK

Test Two

Answers

1. 14

2. Vulnerable

3. Wednesday

4. In the pink

5. Antipodean

6. Rise to vote sir

7. B

8. 7, 21, 22

9. Sack oboe = bookcase. The books are lexicon (Neil Cox), thesaurus (assure hut), omnibus (sumo bin) and cookery (Roy Coke)

10. Modest

11. Fox

12. 14; $14^2 = 196$

13. Halt, start

14. B; A is the same as E rotated, and C is the same as D

15. Fresh – water – fall – short – story – line – age – group

16. 28, 102; $7 \times 4 = 28$, $74 + 28 = 102$

17. Pen; it is a female swan. The rest are all male animals

18. Picture-gallery

19. 2,4; 24336 × 2 = 48672, ie the number formed at the top half of the decagon is double the number formed by the bottom half

20. Exultation

21. 26676; arrange the digits so that the last three digits form a number that is the square of the first two digits

22. O

23. B

24. Predetermine

25. 35; the middle three digits are obtained by dividing the number at the top by 5, the number bottom left by 3, and the number bottom right by 4

26. Tile 3B is incorrect and should be replaced by Tile C

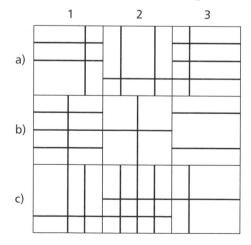

27. C

28. Libretto; libretto is the words of a musical composition, the rest are types of song

29. 48

30. Keen – enthusiastic

31. 27; (2 × 9) + 9
Similarly; (3 × 4) + 9 = 21 and (7 × 6) + 3 = 45

32. 8 4 D F K L N P Q T Z 3 5 7

33. C; the sequence progresses black/line, two blacks/line, three blacks/line which is then repeated with white alternatively black circles

34. Kidnap, theft

35. 43; in each line across multiply the first and third numbers, then add 1 to obtain the number in the middle

36. 93 and 92 should be swapped round
The top sequence progresses −1, −2, −1, −2, −1
The bottom sequence progresses −2, −1, −2, −1, −2

37. Synonyms: accuse, cite
Antonym: absolve

38. 1 foot; sapling = 1 foot, wall = 7 foot

39. In good nick

40. B; so that the sequence is palindromic ie the same symbols appear when read back to front

Test Three

Answers

1. Paragraph; the vowel is O

2. Jacksonville

3. D; each time two symbols touch they disappear at the next stage and are replaced by two new symbols

4.

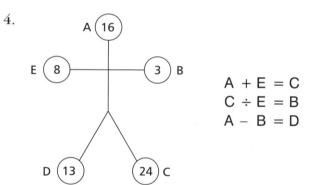

$$A + E = C$$
$$C \div E = B$$
$$A - B = D$$

5. Auld Lang Syne

6. I scream, ice cream

7. 18; 14 × 4 = 56,   4 × 4 = 16,   8 × 4 = 32
       9 × 4 = 36,   7 × 4 = 28,   5 × 4 = 20

8. One man band; to give: ago, fan, hue, dim, lea, pan, hob, pea, man, wad.

9. Embroidery (my dire robe)

10. B; flag

11. E; all the others are made up of three identical shapes

12. Supplication, plea

13. –2; 1 (+1) = 2, 2 (–2) =   0
        0 (+3) = 3, 3 (–4) = –1
       –1 (+5) = 4, 4 (–6) = –2

14. The Old Man and the Sea (Ernest Hemingway); to give: hothead, scolded, romance, slander, dithery, roseate

15. 4; the numbers represent the number of consonants in each word of the question

16. E;   the black circle moves one left, three right
         the line moves one right, three left
         the tower moves two left, one right
         the white circle moves one right, two left

17. RUE; each letter moves forward three places in the alphabet:

O P Q R
R S T U
B C D E

18. 45; 13 × 4 = 52 – 7 = 45

19. Lax/lacks

20. Avoid

21. 10; in each set, each horizontal and vertical line of three numbers adds up to 16

22. Synonyms: lugubrious, rueful
    Antonym: pleased

23. 48
    48 + 8 = 56
    48 − 20 = 28

24. Glass, granite

25. B; the arrows are pointing away from the face

26. 5967; in all the other numbers the digits progress +4, +1, −3

27. Lullaby, ditty, serenade

28.

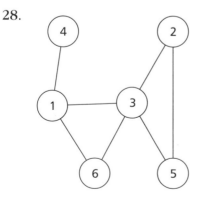

29. P

30. B; the three different symbols are being arranged in groups of three in every possible order ie in six possible combinations

31. B

32. 42 days
7 men take 30 days, therefore, one man would take 210 days
$210 \div 5$ men $= 42$ days

33. Maintain, conclude

34. C

35. Presbytery; it is a building for clergy. The rest are teaching establishments

36. Poultice

37. 32 and 31 should be swapped round
The top sequence progresses: $+4, +8, +4, +8, +4, +8$
The bottom sequence progresses: $+8, +4, +8, +4, +8, +4$

38. 2; in the first block diagonally opposite digits total 14, in the second block they total 15 and in the third block 16

39. Exemplify, epitomize

40. C; at each stage the dots move $45°$ clockwise and another dot is added at the end. The dots added alternate white/black

Test Four

Answers

1. Clarion; all the others have a keyboard

2. At a loss for words

3. 46284; take the even numbers in reverse order

4. None of them repeat a letter

5. D; there are three different top symbols and three different bottom (inverted) symbols in each horizontal line and vertical column of shields

6. Molecule, particle

7. C; mansard : roof

8. Folly

9. 9, 11; start at the top right-hand square and spiral to the centre following the route shown in the sequence –2, +1, +2

7	5	4	6	START
5	8	10	8	
6	9	11	7	
8	6	7	9	

10. They can all be prefixed with semi, ie semiprecious, semicircle, semitone, semi-automatic

11. Keep the ball rolling

12. 8; the top three lines added together equal the bottom line: 27684 + 12196 + 25478 = 65358

13. 13211A; each group describes the one before, ie one 3, two 1s, one A

14.

D	A	M	P			
A	R	E	A			
M	E	W	S			
P	A	S	T	I	M	E
			I	D	O	L
			M	O	S	S
			E	L	S	E

15. C; one is a mirror image of the other

16. Evacuation; it repeats the letter a. All the other words have the vowels a, e, i, o, u, once only

17. 7984; in all the others multiply the middle two digits to obtain the first and fourth digits, for example 5964, where 9 × 6 = 54

18. Knavish, principled

19. Thunder storm, to give: hat, hen, pad, rue, ear, sit, elm

20. Martin, which is an anagram of Antrim
Strode is an anagram of Dorset; milk, rice an anagram of Limerick; and Edna, beer an anagram of Aberdeen

21. 4.55 cm
(10.5 ÷ 7.5) × 3.25

22. Ellipse, ring

23. B

24. ANEDIT = detain

25. 0; each block of four numbers totals 21

26. Elixir of life

27. Condone; it means to forgive or overlook. The rest are to find not guilty

28. A

29. 432 and 648 should be swapped round
    The top sequence progresses x2, x3, x2, x3, x2, x3
    The bottom sequence progresses x3, x2, x3, x2, x3, x2

30. Gaudily

31. A; subtract 1 from all the even numbers and add 1 to all the odd numbers

32. Combine the contents of the first two tiles in each row and column; however, cancel out any circles that appear in the same tile twice

33. Claustrophobia

34. A; lines across progress +1, +2, +1. Lines down progress +5, +8, +5

35. A E U 8 6 5 3 Z P N M K G

36. 12

37. Synonyms: surplus, glut
    Antonym: paucity

38. D; the sequence of eight symbols is being repeated and every third symbol is twice the size of the rest

39. £2,500
    35% = 7/20 and 3/5 = 12/20 ie 19/20 in total
    Carrie's share of £125 must, therefore, be 1/20
    Total sum of money, therefore, is £125 × 20 = £2,500

40. C; the third line is the first line in reverse and the fourth line is the second line in reverse

Test Five

Answers

1. 14

2. Enable, length, thieve, vendor, oracle, lessen

3. 1.5 minutes

$$\frac{1}{3} + \frac{1}{2} - \frac{1}{6} = 0.33 + 0.5 - 0.166 = 0.66$$

$$\frac{1}{0.66} = 1.5 \text{ minutes}$$

4. B; the large arc moves 45° anti-clockwise. The two remaining arcs move 90° anti-clockwise

5. Tap; all the other three-letter words are spelt out by alternate letters of one of the seven-letter words, for example ASTOUND = SON

6. 53; $3 + 2 = 5$ $2 + 1 = 3$

7. They all contain Biblical characters:
   ABUN(DAN)CE, AL(LEVI)ATE, UNT(RUTH)S, PRO(CAIN)E, C(HAM)BER

8. P; there are 15 letters before it in the alphabet, and ten after

9. Flush toilet

10. C; it repeats the second flag with left and right reversed in the same way that the third flag repeats the first flag

11.

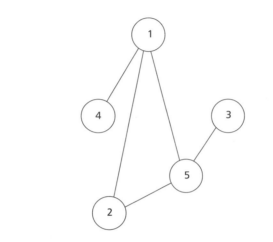

12. Fragrant, aromatic

13. Simpler tax

14. D; invent

15. Meet – encounter (truce none)

16. 698; the numbers 98725136 are being repeated in the same order

17. Professional

18. 27; there are two sequences running alternately. The first starts with 7 and goes +2, +3, +4 etc. The second starts with 8 and goes +2, +4, +6 etc

19. Vagrant, itinerant

20. Put on ice

21. 13762; in all the others divide the number formed by the first three digits by 3 to obtain the number formed by the last two digits

22. Senate, temple, legacy, cymbal, allege, genial, allude, defuse

23. 20

24. 33 and 34 should be swapped round
The top sequence progresses +3, +6, +9, +12, +15
The bottom sequence progresses +4, +5, +6, +7, +8

25. Bitter, effortless

26. 1550 (62 ÷ 4) × 100

27. D

28. BETTER RAVE = vertebrate
The reptiles are alligator (at gorilla), chameleon (clean home), crocodile (cool cider) and basilisk (ski bails)

29. Synonyms: supreme, omnipotent
Antonym: weak

30. D; looking at lines across, the dot moves one corner clockwise at each stage. Looking at columns down, the dot is moving one corner anti-clockwise at each stage

31. B

    ←←→↓↕↕↔→↑←←→↕←←→↓↕↕↔→↑←←
    →↕←←→↓(↕)↕↔→↑←←→↕←←→↓↕↕↔→↑
    ←←→↕←←→↓↕↕↔→↑←←→↕

32. 46; add 7, 2, 9 repeated

33. Report

34. 5; $6 \times 8 = 48$, $9 \times 7 = 63$, therefore, $5 \times 9 = 45$

35. R

36. Each line across and down contains a centre dot. Looking at lines across the line moves 45° clockwise at each stage. Looking down it moves 45° anti-clockwise

37. B; C contains the same symbols as D, and A contains the same symbols as E

38. C; start the second row with the same number but then add successive numbers on the top row to obtain the numbers at the bottom ie $9 + 2 = 11$, $11 + 6 = 17$, $17 + 3 = 20$, $20 + 7 = 27$, $27 + 5 = 32$

39. T S P M L K F 9 5 2 6 8

40. Lustrous, polished

Test Six

Answers

1. Fluvial/river, psittacine/parrot, corvid/rook, vernal/spring

2. 7662; start at 56 and work clockwise as follows:
   + 1 × 2, + 2 × 2, + 3 × 2, + 4 × 2 etc.
   For example (56 + 1) × 2 = 114, (114 + 2) × 2 = 232

3. D; only circles connected to one other circle are carried
   forward and a line is then drawn between them

4. 6814; reverse the digits and add together to obtain the
   final digits

5. Crush, break

6. Caretaker

7. 23; discard the highest digit each time, then reverse the
   remaining digits

8. MOMS HOUR = MUSHROOM. The animals are: springbok
   (brisk pong), chipmunk (punch Kim), leopard (red opal)
   and buffalo (fab foul)

9. R; only letters with an enclosed area are printed

10. Lineage

11. A dog! A panic in a pagoda

12. 11

13. E; the two lines are moving one corner at a time at each stage, one clockwise, the other anti-clockwise

14. Faithful

15.

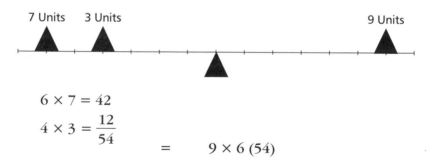

$6 \times 7 = 42$

$4 \times 3 = \dfrac{12}{54}$

$= \quad 9 \times 6 \, (54)$

16. Oscillated

17. B; A is the same as D with black/white reversal
C is the same as E with black/white reversal

18. On the level

19. 14; 7 × 4 = 28 ÷ 2 = 14

20. E; aphelion

21. 1; 21 × 4 = 84. Similarly 26 × 3 = 78 and 17 × 5 = 85

22. Clandestine *collection* of vital information that cannot be obtained by any *overt* means requires the recruitment of agents who are able to obtain the *required* intelligence without *detection*

23. 9 5 B J K N P T Z 2 4 6 8

24. 86 and 81 should be swapped round
The top sequence progresses: +15, +18, +15, +18, +15, +18
The bottom sequence progresses: +12, +15, +12, +15, +12, +15

25. Stalk, flower

26. A; the figure at the top rotates 45° and goes in the middle of the figure at the bottom, which rotates 90°. The figure in the middle rotates 90° and goes to the top

27. David 68, George 102

28. Synonyms: pleasant, amiable
Antonym: impolite

29. E; it contains a repeated symbol. The rest all contain a set of different symbols

30. Surfeit – plethora

31. 950 minutes = 15 hours 50 minutes
    Train = 39 minutes. Bus = 56 minutes. 39 × 5 days =
    195 minutes. 56 × 5 days = 280 minutes. Return journey
    = (195 × 2) + (280 × 2) = 950 minutes

32. D

33. E

34. D; add the digits of each number on the top row to obtain
    the number below it

35. Enumerator

36. ABDICATE

37. A

38. 14; add the odd numbers only

39. Integer; it is a whole number. The rest are all parts which
    divide into other numbers

40. 53; the numbers in the middle section are the average of
    the numbers either side

Test Seven

Answers

1. A; there are two alternate sequences. In the first the circles are getting smaller, in the second they are getting larger

2. Starting post; to give: cut, tea, oat, ran, pep, ass

3. Dumbfounded; in each word the letters ONE are moving up one place, ie
   . O . N . E . . . ., . . O . N . E . . . . etc

4. 6; the number in the first triangle is arrived at by adding the numbers at the top, ie 6 + 3 + 8 − 17. Similarly, 7 + 8 + 9 = 24, and 2 + 3 + 1 = 6

5. Let testing client

6. 25 appears twice, 57 is missing

7. Appealing

8. 4; the total of numbers on each side is 26

9. XYZ = CAT; cattle, scathe, locate, muscat

10. B; at each stage the dot moves down one. After it has appeared in a figure, that figure becomes inverted

11. C A P R I C O R N
    A P R I C O T
  D E P R I V E
    S L I V E R
   L I B R A
Variations are possible

12. Call it a day

13. Season, sonnet

14. Feeble

15. Monday; skip an extra day at each stage

16. E; each triangle stays on its same base but its apex moves.
The triangle with the dot moves one clockwise, two anti-
clockwise etc. The other triangle moves in exactly the
same way

17. Move as follows:

8	5	3
6	T	1
4	2	7

18. Known ocean, no notion

19. Considerably

20. All contain a drink:

    TOT(AL E)CLIPSE
    A PI(G IN) A POKE
    WHI(TE A)DMIRALS

21. 6; the numbers along the first row increase by 4, the numbers along the second row decrease by 2 and the numbers along the third row increase by 4

22. Part, whole

23. D; the sequence consists of the repeated symbols
    ╬ ╥ ╣ ╠ ╚ ╝ ╞ ╪ ╝

24. Joe 16, Mo 20, Flo 25

25. Saffron; the rest are all sweeteners

26. C; every second circle has a vertical line, every third circle has a black dot, every fourth circle has a horizontal line and every fifth circle has a diagonal line

27. 37 and 38 should be swapped round
    The top sequence progresses +13, +15, +17, +19, +21
    The bottom sequence progresses +11, +14, +17, +20, +23

28. 4248; $6 \times 1 \times 7 = 42$ and $3 \times 8 \times 2 = 48$

29. A Dutch inventor Cornelius van Drebbel managed to build a type of submarine in 1620. He wrapped a wooden rowboat tightly in waterproof *leather* and fused air *tubes* with *floats* reaching to the surface to provide oxygen

30. The greatest possible area will be in the form of a square. Each side will be 58 yards long (232 ÷ 4). Its area will be 58 × 58 = 3364 square yards

31. Inveighed, invade

32. D

33. Synonyms: trim, spruce
    Antonym: bedraggled

34. C; the rest contain the same seven symbols

35. 15 boxes
    270 × 2 = 540 shoes. 15 × 36 = 540

36. D; looking from top line to bottom line each line moves 45° clockwise

37. 8 6 2 3 5 7 9 W V T S R P N K J F E D

38. 41; (4 × 8) + 9

39. Frontispiece

40. Eloquent, hesitant

Test Eight

Answers

1. EMRUD = DEMUR

2. 2; the numbers in each circle add up to 33

3. Rainstorm (minor arts)

4. Sistine Chapel; to give: obi, was, eat, own, fee, lac, dip, ode, nil

5. C; the top apex and the bottom right apex are folded over

6. 20 minutes; $30 \times \dfrac{10}{15}$

7. 5

8. Defeatist

9. D; the figures outside the square move from the 12 o'clock to the 9 o'clock position. The circle goes in the middle of the square and the other figure half inside the square

10. Terminal, velocity

11. Crook, cheat

12. Overt

13. 26; add 3, 4, 5, 6 then 7

14. A penny for your thoughts

15. Mogul; it is an Indian dynasty. The rest are Chinese

16. E; words

17. 6; in the first circle opposite segments total 7, in the second circle they total 8, and in the third circle 9

18. SHA; Marsha, Sharon

19. A; at each stage the black circle moves one segment anti-clockwise, then two segments, then three etc. The white circle does the same, but clockwise

20. B; A is a mirror image of D and C a mirror image of E

21. Y

22. B; the dots in the middle circle comprise of the top dot from the top left-hand circle, the left-hand dot from the top-right circle, the bottom dot from the bottom-left circle and the right dot from the bottom-right circle

23. 18 and 17 should be swapped round
The top sequence progresses ×2 – 1 repeated
The bottom sequence progresses ×2 – 2 repeated

24. Reckless, cautious

25. 98

$$\frac{277}{554} = \frac{1}{2} \frac{1^2}{2} = \frac{1}{4} \frac{1}{4} \times 392 = 98$$

26. Lunar, sidereal

27. D; B is the same as E in reverse and A is the same as C in reverse

28. 2; multiply all the numbers together to obtain the next number in the sequence

29. Verity, canard

30. 89; 32 + 57

31. F; reversing the first analogy, the dot inside top moves to outside right, the dot inside left moves to outside top, the dot inside bottom moves to inside left and the dot outside bottom moves to outside left

32. Advertisement; it is a general term, the rest are specific types of advertising leaflets

33. 10
    3 numbers = 26 × 3 = 78
    2 numbers = 34 × 2 = 68
    The third number is 78 – 68 = 10

34. A; the sequence progresses — ▼ —— ▲ ——— ▶ ——
    —— ◀ which is repeated except that the number of triangles increase from one to two

35.

 2 . 357
   24 . 8
    4 . 75
 329 . 6
 361 . 507

36.
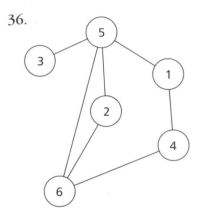

37. Synonyms: reproach, carp
    Antonym: extol

38. B

39. Strait, straight

40. 5; the top row plus the second row equals the third row
    ie 269 + 547 = 816 and 758 + 196 = 954

Test Nine

Answers

1. D; opposite segments are a mirror image of each other

2. Ordinary, inspired

3. Esoteric

4. D; black circles turn to white diamonds; white circles turn to black diamonds, and vice versa

5. 1; reading clockwise $89 + 54 = 143$
    $$98 + 31 = 129$$
    $$84 + 87 = 171$$

6. Plum pie, plump eye

7. All contain internal palindromes; p(refer)able, purv(eye)d, tara(did)dle, bag(pip)es, bej(ewe)lled

8. Blessed, cursed

9. A;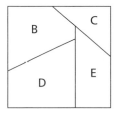

10. B; looking both across and down the contents of the third tile is determined by the contents of the first two tiles. Lines are carried forward except when a line appears in both tiles, in which case it is cancelled out

11. Elate; the rest are anagram pairs: glean/angle, riled/idler, horse/shore, groan/organ, caned/dance, eager/agree, owned/endow, broth/throb

12. LAND = 91; nine straight lines, one curved

13. K; start at the bottom left square and travel up and down columns to read 'snakes and ladders'

14. E; all the rest are the same figure rotated

15. Indirect, straight

16. Starting-point

17. F

18. D; $68 + 93 = 161$

19. Damson; to give: bid, lea, ham, his, too, fan

20. 8; $3 \times 8 = 24 - 6 = 18$

21. Synonyms: plush, palatial
    Antonym: spartan

22. E; the sequence consists of the repeated symbols
▶▼▲◀▼▶▲▶◀▼
and every fourth symbol is twice as big as the rest

23. BRIGHT and EARLY

24. 88 and 90 should be swapped round
The top sequence progresses: –1, –2, –3, –4, –5
The bottom sequence progresses –2, –4, –6, –8, –10

25. Z T P N L K G F 3 7 9 U E A 8 6

26. B

27. D; the rest are palindromic, ie they read the same backwards and forwards

28. 9
The rule is to replace – – with │ .
– 16 + 25 = +9

29. Tile 1C is incorrect and should be replaced by Tile D

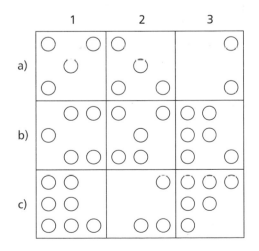

30. Apricot; the rest are citrus fruits

31. B; add 1 to pairs of diagonally opposite numbers ie in the left-hand set 7 – 5 becomes 6 – 8

32. Pursuance

33. 21 units
    by Pythagoras:
    $$35^2 = 1225$$
    $$\text{less }\ 28^2 = \ \underline{784}$$
    $$\sqrt{441} = 21$$

34. Part; departed, repartee, apartment, impartial

35. 202; the sequence progresses $\times 3 + 1$ repeated

36. F; A is the same as E with black/white reversal. Similarly B=G and D=C

37. £38

38. RRRR + AEEFGIOT = refrigerator

39. 733; deduct the middle digit each time to obtain the next number

40. Wistful, solicitous

Test Ten

Answers

1. 5246; in the others the middle number is half of the number formed by the first and last digits, eg 3186 (36/2 = 18)

2. Circumvent

3. C; the figure at the top goes to the bottom. The figure inside the larger figure at the bottom rotates through 90° and goes to the top. The larger figure at the bottom reduces in size and goes inside the figure now at the top

4. Eradicate, eliminate

5. Eternity ring

6. C; it contains the black dot and one smaller white circle inside the large circle, and one smaller white circle and black circle partly inside the large circle

7. Charmingly

8. B; the smallest number is discarded at each stage and the remaining numbers travel in the opposite direction to the previous stage

9. E; so one dot is in one circle and the other dot is in the circle and ellipse

10. 2; 7 + 8 + 8 = 23

11. Eventful, ordinary

12. 117; alternately subtract, then add the sum of the digits of the previous number

13. A; the triangles become one large triangle and the truncated ellipse becomes two, rotating 180° and going inside the triangle

14. Sleigh ride

15. Loom

16. Chivalrous

17. C; at each stage one of the sections goes through 45° and continues to move 45° at subsequent stages

18. 6; add 0.5, 1, 1.5, 2

19. DEPNU = UPEND

20. Take the top circle on the left with the bottom circle on the right, etc, to spell out beard, heard, heart, learn, pearl, weary and yearn, with the addition of EAR

21. Lines across progress +2, +3, +1, +2, +1
    Lines down progress +5, +1, −2, +1, −3

1	3	6	7	9	10
6	8	11	12	14	15
7	9	12	13	15	16
5	7	10	11	13	14
6	8	11	12	14	15
3	5	8	9	11	12

22. Synonyms: cynical, sceptical
    Antonym: gullible

23. Env(iron)ment

24. D; the middle figure changes to a diamond and rotates
    90°. The outer figure reduces its number of sides by 1

25. Zinc; the rest are alloys

26. Filter, simmer

27. 3 5 7 Z Y X T P L K J F E C 4 2

28. B

☺ ♣ ♫ — • — ♀ & ($ # @) ☺ ♣ ♫ — • — ♀ & $ # @ ☺ ♣
♫ — • — ♀ & $ # @ ☺ ♣ ♫ — • — ♀ & $ # @ ☺ ♣ ♫ — •
— ♀ & $ # @ ☺ ♣ ♫ — • — ♀ & $ # @ ☺ ♣ ♫ — • — ♀ &
$ # @ ☺ ♣ ♫ — • — ♀ & $ # @ ☺ ♣ ♫ — • — ♀

29. Durable; it is long, the rest are short

30. 60 and 62 should be swapped round
    The top sequence progresses +22, +25, +22, +25, +22, +25
    The bottom sequence progresses +20, +22, +24, +26, +28, +30

31. Name; enamel, ornament

32. Catholic; it means broad-minded. The rest mean narrow-minded

33. 24; divide each number by 8 to obtain the digits in the middle ie $16 \div 8 = 2$ and $32 \div 8 = 4$

34. 53265

35. Esplanade

36. E; the trapezium moves 90° clockwise. The dot moves from corner to corner in turn, also clockwise, and alternates white/black

37. D; the sequence consists of the repeated set of symbols: ♂♂♠♠♪♫☺☺

38. 6

39. C

40. 1; the first column minus the second column equals the third column
    $592 - 379 = 213$
    $815 - 698 = 117$